FOOLPROOF

WOOD FINISHING

FOR THOSE WHO LOVE TO BUILD & HATE TO FINISH

FOOLPROOF
WOOD FINISHING

FOR THOSE WHO LOVE TO BUILD & HATE TO FINISH

BY TERI MASASCHI

Fox Chapel Publishing
1970 Broad Street • East Petersburg, PA 17520
www.FoxChapelPublishing.com

Acknowledgments

Thanks to Lisa, Leanne, Morgan Estill, Steve and Donna Neumon, all of my students, and to my biggest fan, Wingate Paine, for all of the support and encouragement in wood finishing, in undertaking this book, and in life. You made it all possible.

Special thanks to Joseph M. Cupertino Jr. at Leonards New England for supplying the slant-front desk photo on page 187.

Joseph M. Cupertino Jr.
Leonards New England
600 Taunton Ave.
Seekonk, MA 02771
1-888-336-8585
(508) 336-8585
www.leonardsdirect.com

Alan Giagnocavo
Publisher

Peg Couch
Acquisition Editor

Gretchen Bacon
Editor

Troy Thorne
Design

Wil Younger
Layout

Morgan Estill
Interior Photography

Foolproof Wood Finishing is an original work, first published in 2006 by Fox Chapel Publishing Company, Inc. No part of this book may be duplicated for resale or distribution under any circumstances. Any such copying is a violation of copyright law.

ISBN-13: 978–1–56523–303–4
ISBN-10: 1–56523–303–4

Publisher's Cataloging-in-Publication Data

Masaschi, Teri.
    Foolproof wood finishing : for those who love to build & hate to finish / by Teri Masaschi. -- East Petersburg, PA : Fox Chapel Publishing, c2006.
        p. ; cm.

        ISBN-13: 978-1-56523-303-4
        ISBN-10: 1-56523-303-4
        Includes index.

        1. Wood finishing--Technique. 2. Furniture finishing--Technique. 3. Finishes and finishing. I. Title.

TT325 .M37 2006
684.1--dc22   0610

To learn more about the other great books from Fox Chapel Publishing, or to find a retailer near you, call toll-free 1-800-457-9112 or visit us at *www.FoxChapelPublishing.com*.

Note to Authors: We are always looking for talented authors to write new books in our area of woodworking, design, and related crafts. Please send a brief letter describing your idea to Peg Couch, Acquisition Editor, 1970 Broad Street, East Petersburg, PA 17520.

Printed in China
10 9 8 7 6 5 4 3 2 1

Preface

The pace of our society leaves many of us longing for a pursuit without a deadline, one where "it isn't done until it's done right." That longing has led many of us to woodworking and wood finishing. An escape to the shop is an escape from a boss, from power meetings, and from an appointment calendar, even if we do it for a living.

But it's not an escape from discipline. It raises discipline, self-imposed discipline, to a new and satisfying high. It's the discipline, the diligent adherence to proven procedure, that leads to legitimate satisfaction, and hopefully to perfection. There are no shortcuts!

The self-imposed discipline of finishing has been the most consistent thread through my life, ever since I was 14. I have prepared my surfaces, applied the colors, spread the coatings, and polished to a beautiful sheen, over and over again—but seldom without "diffoogulties," as an old Yankee who knew about such things used to put it. There have been scars that can't be sanded out, uneven color, pools and sags in an otherwise flawless exterior, and worn-out spots from too much polishing. We call it "finishing," but we practice it repeatedly to get better at it. Nothing is ever truly finished! It's a strikingly accurate metaphor for life, at least for my life.

—Teri

About the Author

Author Teri Masaschi has built, restored, conserved, and refinished furniture for nearly four decades. She learned how to restore antiques and refinish wood, as well as how to build Queen Anne, Federal, and Chippendale furniture, as a 14-year-old apprentice for a New Hampshire fine arts dealer. The experience sparked a lifetime passion for the work that has never faded.

After three decades as a professional finisher/refinisher specializing in antique restoration and reproduction, she left New Hampshire and moved to New Mexico to become finishing specialist/product manager for Woodworker's Supply Inc. Today she runs her own finishing and restoration business in Tijeras, New Mexico, and shares her exhaustive knowledge of simple and advanced finishing techniques and ways to maintain and restore antiques with students at woodworking schools around the country, including the prestigious Center for Furniture Craftsmanship in Rockport, Maine, and Anderson Ranch Arts Center in Snowmass, Colorado. She is also a frequent contributor to *Fine Woodworking* magazine.

CONTENTS

Introduction

Most woodworkers are not finishers. It is nothing to be upset about; woodworking and finishing demand different skills. But many of those who are not finishers want to become finishers. When they start to look into it, they come right up against the fantastic array of finishing products on the market, and that "curse of riches" makes learning wood finishing somewhat complicated. In woodworking, if a router bit is an ogee-style bit, that's it—very straightforward. But in finishing, a stain is not just a stain. It could be oil- or alcohol- or water-based, dye or pigment or both, gel or penetrating or glaze. Choosing among the alternatives is never just black or white; advantages come with disadvantages. Some who've struggled call finishing a "black art"!

On the other hand, if you take the time to dive into this "dark" world and learn about the various products, it can be very exciting. You'll begin to develop a feeling of control over the outcome of your projects when you realize that stain doesn't have to go on raw wood. That feeling will grow as you complete each of the step-by-step exercises in the book. And therein lies the whole point of the book—learn the processes without taking risks by making your mistakes on scrap instead of on your woodworking project.

How to use this book

In the first chapter, we'll cover some of the basics of finishing, including tools and materials, safety, and the first of the three stages of finishing: planning. The step-by-step exercises, which make up the majority of the book, show you how to perform the second stage of finishing: making test samples. In other words, you'll finish stock from your project to make sure you'll get the results you anticipate. Completing the exercises will prepare you for the final stage of finishing: completing your project. Finally, we'll finish up with some information on the care of your carefully finished projects.

The upcoming chapters follow the same sequence as finishing: preparing the surface, filling holes, grain filling, coloring, topcoating, rubbing out, and finally repairing and touching up. However, you don't need to complete every exercise in the book. Some finishes, for example, won't require you to fill grain or use color. I suggest that you take a look at the finishes that interest you, read through the demonstrations carefully, and then decide which exercise(s) you want to tackle.

You'll find a tools and materials list at the beginning of each group of exercises as well as additional materials and tools for each exercise. The supply list at the back of the book will help you find the products that you will need and my preferred brands. Remember to stick within the recommended usage, dry time, and directions from the manufacturer—and be sure to have fun and be brave!

Beyond this book

The big picture of finishing is much more than this book. Once you have completed some or even all of these exercises, you will have only scratched the surface (pardon the expression). In the world of factory finishing, it gets quite sophisticated with large conveyors, drums of coatings attached to spray guns, in-line, automated spray systems, UV ovens to force dry the finishes, and more. The huge investment adds only one element missing in our hand applied finishes: efficiency. The factory follows the same general sequence as hand application—surface prep, colorants, sealing, glazing, and topcoating—but it does it at many times the speed. Instead of dry times taking days it only needs hours. Wow!

When I teach finishing there are always 2 or 3 out of a group of 12 to 14 who are "spray heads." They want to move quickly into the fast lane and learn the art of spray finishing. It's a handy skill if you are in business, if you are incredibly impatient, or if you simply want to acquire more tools! But it's an expensive proposition; the guns, the spray booth, the clean room, the investment in industrial coatings all cost money. It's quite a commitment. But the efficiency and consistent quality from a well-run spray room are awesome. There are some finishing shops that put out a satin gun finish (a finish right off the gun with no rub-out) that is superior to a hand applied satin finish that has been rubbed out.

If you hunger to learn more finishing and faster finishing (and of course the opportunity to shop for more tools) seek out an instructor or a school that specializes in it: finishing school. Or you can do it my way—37 years of falling into every pitfall and learning how to back out of them. I've heard that this is what they call an expert! Remember, you have to start before you finish.

Good Finishing,

Teri

Getting Started

. . . .

While we'll be spending a good deal of time in this book going over the how-tos of finishing, it's extremely important to begin any finishing project by planning what you want to do. You'll need to determine the best finish for your particular project and how you will go about accomplishing it. This chapter will cover all of those important basics for planning a finish as well as some other principles, such as tool selection and safety, that will help you pick the best methods for working safely and efficiently. By changing your mindset and practicing a more proactive approach to finishing, you will be in the driver's seat instead of the can of stain!

Assessing the project

The most important part of finishing starts at the very beginning of the project at the drafting table when the piece is being drawn and the cut list generated. On your project designs, leave room for planning out the finish. Begin by asking yourself the following questions:

What is the function of the piece?

Will it need a super-durable topcoat?

Will it have a special color to match?

Will some parts need prefinishing?

If the piece is built from random boards (not all from the same tree), what risks are there with color inconsistency?

If there are sap streaks (white streaks), is it necessary to cut them out, plan around them, or plan on coloring them in?

Is the piece going to be made from wood that is prone to "blotching"?

These questions will lead you to the features you'll need to consider when choosing a finish for your piece. Most considerations relate to either function or appearance. Let's look at some of these features in greater detail.

Function

The function of the piece is very important to keep in mind. How will the piece be used? Will it be used on a daily basis (a kitchen table, a chest at the end of a bed, or a bench in an entryway on which to sit and put on your shoes)? Will it simply be decorative? Asking yourself these questions will ultimately lead you to the characteristics of the appropriate finish.

Most often, the characteristics determined by function involve durability and a project's resistance to movement, heat, and other environmental factors. To get the outward protection you need for the piece, you'll want to choose the appropriate topcoat.

Topcoating serves two purposes: it provides the surface texture and sheen of the piece, and it is the primary defense against wear and tear. If your project will be used on a daily basis, the finish needs to be a durable polyurethane. If the project is completely decorative, like a jewelry box or a picture frame, a finish like shellac would be perfect because it is quite beautiful but doesn't rate very highly in durability.

For pieces that will be particularly susceptible to wood movement, such as a frame and panel construction, the type of finish you choose as well as prefinishing, or finishing before assembly, can be particularly important. Prefinishing parts like raised panels prevents exposing uncolored edges when they shrink during the dry season. Panels should be stained and sealed before assembly to prevent a white line along the long edge during the dry season. Shellac is the best choice for sealing up areas such as tabletop bottoms and interiors of drawers and chests.

You'll also want to take repair and touch-up into consideration. Some finishes, such as polyurethane, are very durable but are difficult to touch up if damaged. Solvent-based lacquer, on the other hand, is not as durable but is a breeze to fix should something happen. To help you determine which topcoats suit your needs, I've provided the chart on the next page, which compares the durability and other characteristics of the various finishes. For more information about the various topcoats, see Chapter 5, "Topcoating," on page 91.

Characteristics of Topcoats

Topcoat	Water Resistance	Scuff and Scratch Resistance	Heat Resistance	Appearance	Ability to be Repaired
Shellac, dewaxed, super blond	2	2	1	2	4
Brushing lacquer	3	3	1	3	4
Oil urethane or varnish interior	4	4	2	5	1 or 2
Penetrating oils (Danish)	1	1	0	5	5
Wiping varnishes (gels etc.)	1 or 2 (#of coats)	1 or 2 (#of coats)	1	4	1 or 2
Water-based urethanes	2	3	2	1	3
Waxes, clear	1	1	0	3	5

1 denotes worst, 5 denotes best; for appearance, 1 denotes clearest, 5 denotes most yellowing

Appearance

How you want the finished piece to look determines other qualities of the ideal finish for your piece. Do you want a specific color? Do you prefer the look of natural wood? Is the random appearance of sapwood streaks an eyesore or is it beauty in the eye of the maker? These are all considerations of appearance, and understanding them will aid you in finding the right products. Not surprisingly, many of the requirements for the appearance of your project involve the wood selection as much as they involve the finish.

Wood selection

Color consistency, sapwood streaks, and other peculiar tendencies in wood can be dealt with when standing in front of the lumber rack or at the lumberyard. If the cabinetmaker is a lover of the wood "au naturel" and thinks that these defects are beautiful, then choosing high-quality, consistent wood is not an issue. But for those pieces that require a discriminating choice of stock, such as a formal highboy or a Bombay chest, the wood choice must be high quality.

Natural finishes

Most woodworkers can make their way through some type of a clear coat when no color is involved in the work. However, you still need to know the differences between clear finishes. The most important is the difference between an oil-based coating and a water-based coating. Oil-based varieties are much more amber in tone and continue to yellow over time. Water-based types are completely clear (to the point of being described as "cold") and do not yellow. (For more information on clear topcoats, see Chapter 5, "Topcoating," on page 91.)

If you are using a clear coat, you'll also want to consider what impact your steps of surface preparation will have on the finished piece. Any processes that you perform should blend into the wood naturally because there will be no color to help blend any filling that you've done in the initial stages. (For more on surface preparation, see Chapter 3, "Preparing the Wood," on page 25.)

With most clear coats or topcoats, you can choose a satin or gloss finish. Rubbing out your finish can also help give the final product a more polished, or "finished," look. (For more information on rubbing out finishes, see the Rubbing Out Finishes section on page 120.)

Using color

Coloring is arguably the most dominant visual aspect of a finish. It affects the character of the piece as a whole, and it determines whether the piece will fit comfortably in an existing environment. There are a variety of ways to add color to a piece, whether it's by using premixed paint or stain or by mixing color with another product. Because the ways to add color are numerous, there are several things to consider when you are planning a colored finish.

CHAPTER 1 – GETTING STARTED

You'll first want to consider which products will give you the results you want. Though many woodworkers cringe at the thought of painting a finely crafted project, paint can achieve a variety of effects (unavailable with stains) that will enhance the final piece. Paint is also used when a customer requests it, when the wood is poor quality, or when matching surrounding elements is required. (To learn more about effects with paint, see pages 112 and 113.)

Stains, whether premixed or mixed by hand, can generally be broken down into two categories based on their use of dye or pigment. Here are some characteristics of dyes and pigments to keep in mind when you are choosing products:

Dyes	Pigments
Dissolve in liquid	Settle in liquid
Penetrate wood relatively evenly	Lodge only in large recesses, such as pores and scratches
Are mostly transparent	Tend to obscure wood
Fade more quickly than pigments	Are resistant to fading
	Must be "bound" to wood with a binder

These characteristics will help to point you in the right direction when you begin to choose the method for coloring your piece. (For more information on using color, see Chapter 4, "Coloring Wood," on page 57.)

It's important to remember as you work with colors that your topcoat must not interfere with your coloring product. The Binders and Solvents charts on this page show the common binders and solvents for the different types of stains. Always check the ingredients in the coloring product as well as the topcoat you wish to use before finalizing your finishing plan.

Binders and Solvents for Pigments	
Binder	**Solvent**
Oil	Mineral spirits
Varnish	Mineral spirits
Lacquer	Lacquer thinner
Water-based resin	Water, glycol ether

Binders and Solvents for Dyes	
Binder	**Solvent**
None	Water
None	Alcohol
None	Turpentine, lacquer thinner

You'll also want to take the wood into consideration when you choose a coloring agent. If the wood has defects or if it is prone to blotching, you may want to reconsider the wood choice or know that you will spend some extra time preparing the surface. (Information on surface preparation can be found in Chapter 3, "Preparing the Wood," on page 25.)

If you are matching the color of other pieces that you have not finished yourself, a test sample is critical. If you can't quite match, consider a complementary contrast instead of a match. But do make a sample and a decision at the planning stage—don't leave it up in the air.

Prefinishing considerations can open up some additional possibilities for adding color. They allow you to design with contrasting colors without introducing a second species of wood. The blanket chest shown on page 19 uses both cherry and maple. The same general effect could be achieved by using just maple and staining the framework but not the panels. Some furniture designers introduce "line" by using contrasting applied beads made from a different species of wood, or prestaining the same species.

The test sample

Once you have set the requirements for your finish, you are ready to make a test sample. It's the mantra, the golden rule, the supreme law of finishing: test sample. That's it. Seems quite simple doesn't it? But hardly anyone ever does a test sample. How many disasters or reworks of sanding back down could have been avoided if only a scrap left over from the project could have been saved and a finish sample worked up? Instead, the common approach is to dive in, kamikaze style, and start throwing some stain on a piece. The results are scary. You could spend six months carefully crafting a piece and ruin it in one hour!

A test sample serves a few different purposes. First, if you aren't entirely sure about the finish you've chosen or about which finish you should use, a test sample is a great tool for assessing the choices. Second, it can show you any flaws in the process before you make them on your finished project. This type of test sample can be very basic (see **Figure 1.1**). Sand to the proper grit, try some stain, and then seal and/or topcoat. The goal is to process the sample exactly as the real project will be. Then, there are no ugly surprises.

A test sample can also be more sophisticated. It can be elevated to what is called a "step sample." To make a step sample, tape the board into squares and complete the finishing processes. Each square will illustrate one step in the process in its raw state to show how it should look when it needs to be duplicated in the future. The results of the sample in **Figure 1.2** are three "steps." The first indicates how the board looks with just stain, the second when stained and sealed, and the third "step" when topcoated. On the back of the sample, write the date, the client's name (even if it is your spouse!), and the products used. This sample will give a historical view of the process and allows, at any point in the future, a way to duplicate this particular finish. Of course, when the process is a simple one, it seems redundant, but when the finish becomes more sophisticated with color layers, it is critical to document each layer. As you go through this process, it's important to remember that you may need to produce multiple test samples to get the final step sample with the finish you want.

Figure 1.1. A test sample can be as simple as sanding, staining, and topcoating a panel of wood.

Figure 1.2. A step sample, a more sophisticated test sample, shows the history of a finish through each of its steps.

Helpful Tip

Make your Sample Exact

Remember to treat the sample just as you would the finished project. Be careful not to overwork the sample by sanding more diligently or into higher grits, applying the stain too timidly, or simply fussing with the sample more than is possible when the work is transferred to the real project.

You'll also want to avoid underworking the sample by not sanding enough, which will cause the stain "take" to be terrible and the topcoat to perform poorly (see **Figure 1.3**).

Figure 1.3. Avoid overworking or underworking your sample board. The goal is to replicate the results you'll be able to achieve on the completed project.

Documenting your finishing plan

When you have tested and chosen a finishing schedule, write the specifics on the drawings for the project (see **Figure 1.4**). Don't even cut wood until you have complete plans. That sample and your notes on how you produced it are your finishing plans (see **Figure 1.5**). Remember to include all steps of the finishing process—surface preparation and prefinishing, coloring, topcoating, rubbing out, and repairing and touching up. You may also need to include notes on any requirements for finishing prior to assembly. Let's take a quick look at each of the steps you'll need to consider as you document your step sample.

Surface preparation and prefinishing: The surface preparation you perform will often determine how smoothly the rest of the process will go. Remember to note not only the grits that you used, but also the time that you spent on each grit. (Be sure to see the methods for measuring this on page 28.) Include any hole filling or grain filling in your notes. You'll also want to write down any pieces that you know will require prefinishing and keep detailed notes for those as well.

Coloring: This part may be the one that requires the most detailed notes, especially if you are trying to match a particular color. In addition to brand and type (alcohol-based, oil-based, etc.), be sure to include any ratios you used for mixes and the dry times of the various materials.

Topcoating: As the finishing plan is narrowed down in your notes, take detailed notes about the process of thinning, applying, and cleaning up the topcoat chosen for the project. This way, you will have a historic document for the future decision making of any project as well as the one at hand.

Rubbing out: Be sure to note if the rubbing out will be a simple soft rub-out or a full schedule that relies on seven to ten coats of finish that get leveled and polished.

Repairing and touching up: Documenting the type of colors and the topcoat used in the project will make any touch-up a much easier process because you will know exactly what materials you'll need should something get damaged.

One final bit of advice when planning a finish: Grow—don't try to reinvent yourself all at once. Experience can only be built, step by step, not bought. A couple of new techniques is plenty for a single project. A half-dozen is courting disaster. And remember to try out those couple of new techniques on scrap before using them on your project.

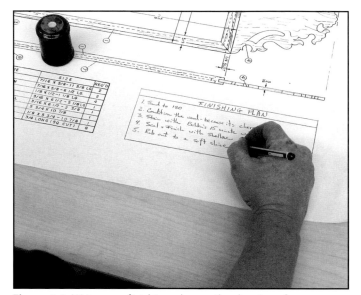

Figure 1.4. Write your finishing plan on the drawings for your project.

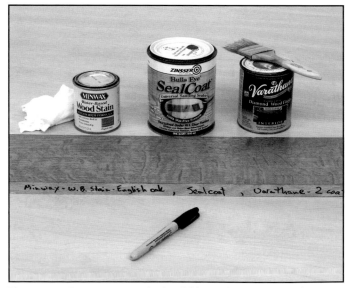

Figure 1.5. Every test sample should have the sequence of materials applied written on the edge or back.

Tools for wood finishing

Compared to woodworking, wood finishing requires very few tools (see **Figure 1.6**). There are brushes that will make your work better. Lighting and clean shop space will improve the environment. The biggest element in finishing is the material that actually finishes the wood. We'll take a quick look at several tool categories here, but be sure to see each chapter for the materials that relate to specific exercises.

Power tools – There are a few power tools that will make finishing a bit easier and less time consuming. A power sander is one of the most useful tools. Power sanding makes short work of what can be a tedious chore. In comparison to hand sanding, in which you are moving one to two hundred strokes per minute, the random orbit sander can move six to eight thousand per minute!

Abrasives – Have a variety of abrasives on hand for sanding and rubbing out some of the different finishes featured in this book. You should have discs for your sander in grit choices from 80 to 220. If you buy in box quantity, the savings are enormous and sandpaper doesn't go bad. You will also need 220 and 320 sheet paper for scuffing. Wet/dry paper in 400 to possibly 2000 grit, depending on the intensity of your rub-outs, is also good to have on hand. The blocks for hand sanding should be made of felt for general sanding and cork or wood for firm sanding that requires leveling.

Cloths/rags – My favorite rags are washed T-shirt material. The worst are any that might be full of lint since these can leave undesirable "fuzzies" in your finish.

Figure 1.6. Tools and materials for finishing may seem numerous to the beginner, but, compared to woodworking, they are very few and inexpensive.

Brushes – Brush choice is fairly simple, partly because the choices are few. For spreading materials like stain and then wiping off the excess with a rag, you don't need a brush that produces a smooth, even coating. Use a cheap brush called a "chip brush." Clean it and re-use it if you want to, but at 50-cents to a dollar per brush, you won't break the bank by using it only once. Chip brushes are made of China bristle, and, if you do much finishing, save a bit of money and a lot of traipsing around by buying them in cases of two or three dozen.

For applying oil-based topcoats and brushing lacquer, use good natural bristle brushes. Traditionally, the best were made from badger bristle, but (like elephant ivory) we don't use that anymore. Even if we legally could, there wouldn't be enough to go around. The brushes called "badger brushes" that you can buy today are made from hog bristle and skunk hair and have the same tapered edge as the traditional badger brush. Another very good natural bristle brush is made with only hog bristle and is commonly called a "lorient brush." A badger or lorient brush costs twenty or more times the cost of a chip brush and is worth taking good care of, as described in the sidebar on pages 10 and 11.

For applying shellac and water-based topcoats, high-quality synthetic brushes like Taklon or J.E. Moser's Choice brushes are a good selection. (Taklon is considered the best synthetic filament for quality brushes.) Such brushes can cost twice the price of a good natural bristle brush. Needless to say, they too are worth taking good care of.

For applying latex paint, get a high-quality brush made specifically for latex paints from a paint store. It should have synthetic flagged bristles that lay out the paint well. Properly cared for, it will last for many years.

Finishing products – The number of finishing products is huge, and we'll be covering a good portion of them in this book. However, the finishing cabinet doesn't need to be filled right away—it will fill rapidly if you purchase products per job or project.

Other household items – In addition to the products specifically related to finishing, you'll also want to have some common household items within reach for many of the exercises. Painter's tape, pencils and permanent markers, finishing nails, stir sticks, disposable cups with ♻ on them (these will not melt with solvents), household ammonia, clean jars from the kitchen or canning jars, old teaspoons and tablespoons, and glue are just some of the items we'll use in this book.

Brushes and their Care

Brush care doesn't need to be a big nuisance if you go about it properly, and if you give the brush good care, it will last for many years. For brush cleaning, one product that you shouldn't do without is Masters Brush Cleaner and Preserver. This product, together with water, removes wet or dry finishing products of all kinds from both synthetic and natural bristle brushes without harming the bristles. It is used widely by artists who can easily have a much bigger investment in brushes than you will.

A final word before we get into cleaning: As a general rule, dedicate a brush to a particular kind of product. That is, even though both oil-based urethane and lacquer use natural bristle brushes, dedicate a brush to oil-based urethane and another to lacquer.

Cleaning finishes from brushes

Figure 1.7. Lacquer thinner helps remove mineral spirits before you clean the brush with Masters Brush Cleaner.

Figure 1.8. Masters Brush Cleaner preserves your investment in a fine brush. It removes virtually all finishes without harming any kind of bristle.

Figure 1.9. Wrapping a damp brush in paper keeps it clean but allows it to dry. Plastic would keep it damp and invite mold.

Oil-Based Urethane

First, submerge the natural bristle brush into the mineral spirits that you used to condition it before you started using it. Swish the excess urethane out of it, and then squeeze out the mineral spirits with a rag. Next, swish the brush in a container with lacquer thinner in it (see **Figure 1.7**). This helps remove the "greasy" spirits. Finally, off to the sink with the brush and the Masters Brush Cleaner. Prime the Masters with a little water in its tub. Swirl the brush in the cleaner and water (see **Figure 1.8**). Begin shampooing the brush with the lather that is worked up in the tub. Clean it thoroughly (maybe two shampoos), and then rinse it under running water. Spin it by hand or whip the brush to remove the excess water. Wrap the brush in paper (not plastic or it will mold) (see **Figure 1.9**). When you use this brush again, it will be soft and just like new.

Water-Based Urethane

Swish the synthetic bristle brush in a mixture of three parts water to one part household ammonia. Then clean it with Masters Brush Cleaner as described above. (Regular dish detergent also works well with water-based finishes.) Wrap the brush in paper or lay it flat on the bench to dry.

Brushing Lacquer

Swish the natural bristle brush in a container of lacquer thinner. Squeeze out the excess in a rag. Then clean it with Masters Brush Cleaner as described above. Shampoo the brush thoroughly, twice if necessary. Knock or spin the excess water out of the brush and wrap it in brown paper.

Latex Paint

Clean as described for water-based urethane, above.

Shellac

This is my favorite; cleaning the brush isn't necessary. Just lay it flat on a clean surface. The brush will tend to harden but will soften up nicely if you let it sit in a cup of shellac for 10 or 15 minutes before its next use. If shellac builds up in the brush, swish it in household ammonia to reduce the excess.

Safety

Safe practices protect your health and the health of your workshop—and your home if the shop is attached. Solvents can harm your skin, lungs, liver, and kidneys if you don't protect them. Many solvents are flammable and some vapors are explosive in sufficient concentrations.

Important as it is, safety does not need to preoccupy your mind every moment that you're finishing wood. It does need to be there in the back of your mind, and it does need to be a work habit. Safety in wood finishing is like safety in driving a car. You acquired safe driving habits during driver training. As an experienced driver, you recognize potentially dangerous situations and avoid the dangers. But you can still enjoy a Sunday afternoon drive in the countryside. Do the same in wood finishing. Develop safe habits including the habit of recognizing potential dangers, and enjoy wood finishing. The most important safety habits follow.

Get and read the Material Safety Data Sheets (MSDS) that outline the hazards of every product that you use (see **Figure 1.10**). The companies that sell these products are required by law to get them to you within 24 hours of a request. They are also commonly available online; do an Internet search for "MSDS."

Ventilate the area. A common approach is to move the stinky air out with a fan. *Stop!* You can't blow air out unless replacement air can come in. If you don't make provisions for clean air to come in, air will sneak in through cracks and crevices and under doors and just about every place where dust and debris collect. That's not quite what you want. If you can't install a ventilation system complete with filtered replacement air, then at least turn the fan around and move clean air *in* (see **Figure 1.11**).

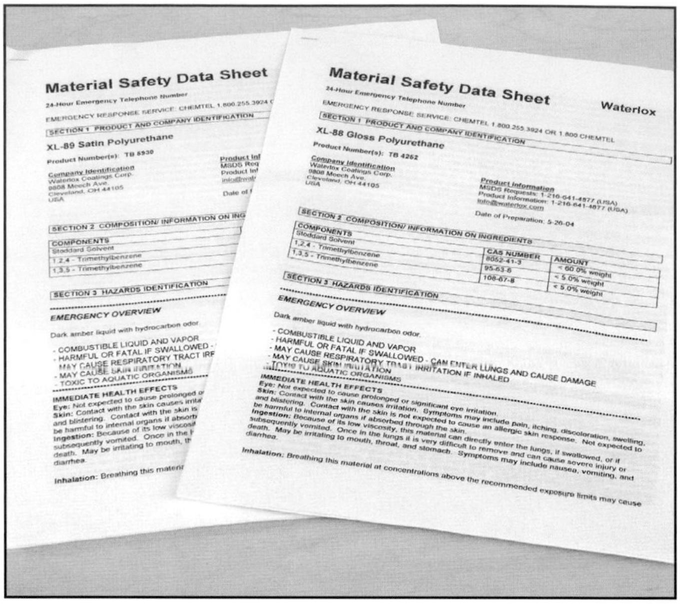

Figure 1.10. Material Safety Data Sheets are your guide to safe product use. Read them.

Figure 1.11. The economy route to ventilation is a fan to move clean air into your shop.

Wear a respirator with fresh cartridges appropriate for the solvents you're using. The cartridges rated for organic vapors deal with most solvents you're likely to use. If you're using full-strength ammonia, order the correct cartridge for it. When you put any new filter on your respirator, it's a good idea to jot the date on the side. Then you'll know how long it has been in use. If you're tempted to postpone replacing a filter, check the cost of replacing a kidney (see **Figure 1.12**).

Wear gloves and protective eyewear. Neoprene is impervious to most of the solvents that are in a finishing shop. Latex and vinyl are not solvent proof but are good for staining because they are less awkward and keep your hands clean. Eyeglasses offer some protection when applying stains and finishes but not enough when pouring or mixing, and goggles are better all the time (see **Figure 1.13**).

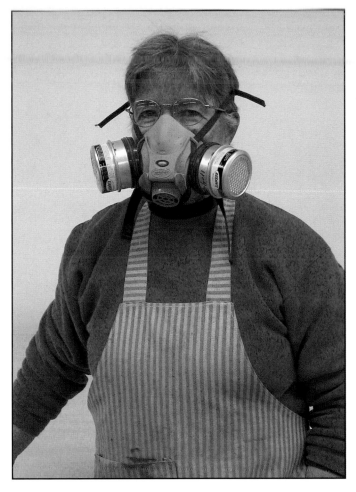

Figure 1.12. A respirator is not a fashion statement, but it will help keep you healthy.

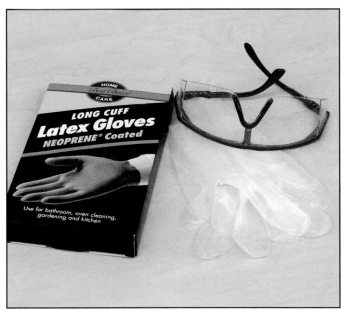

Figure 1.13. Skin and eye protection are well worth their modest cost.

Helpful Tip

Extend the Life of Respirator Cartridges
To lengthen the useful life of a respirator cartridge, keep it sealed in a Ziploc bag when not in use.

Remove oily rags immediately! Left in a pile for as little as 15 or 20 minutes, these rags can spontaneously combust. That means they can start a fire in your shop behind your back or burn it down while you go in the house for a cup of coffee. The oily rag container is the official method (see **Figure 1.14**). The unofficial method is to submerge the rags in a bucket of water until you can hang them out to dry or spread them out on the driveway. When rags are completely dry, they can be thrown out.

Eliminate any source of ignition that fumes could drift to. Such sources include woodstoves, gas appliances, oil-fired boilers and furnaces, and many electric motors. If you have doubts, check if your local fire marshal or fire department offers inspections. And *no smoking!* Need I say more (see **Figure 1.15**)?

Figure 1.14. All oily rags are hazardous. The best way to minimize the hazard is an approved container.

Figure 1.15. Even if you don't, your visitor may. Hang up the sign.

Keep fire extinguishers inspected and located where you will be able to reach them in the event of a fire. An ABC-rated extinguisher is adequate (see **Figure 1.16**).

Solvents are a necessary hazard. Collect used solvents in a safe container, and then get them to a recycling station (**see Figure 1.17**).

Figure 1.16. Keep a fire extinguisher within easy reach of every door to the shop.

Figure 1.17. An open pan of solvent is a source of fumes and a spill waiting to happen. Transfer the solvent to a stable, closable container as soon as you're done using it.

Adventures in Finishing

The most important precaution is to use informed common sense, regardless of how uncommon it is. If it smells bad, feels bad, and looks bad, get out, wash it out, and put it out! Here is a story of some carpenters who didn't.

The beautiful trim work in a house under construction was getting a coat of Watco Danish Oil. The workers finished up and tidied up by piling all the used oily rags in the basement. Then they left. The pile of rags spontaneously combusted, and the resulting fire burned the house down. The owner-attorney sued the maker for not having enough precaution labels on the product. Watco products came off store shelves, the entire line of products was sold to another company, and the new owner provides plenty of warning labels on the product. If the company could, I'm sure it would also provide a small tube of common sense with every can!

A Gallery of Finely Finished Furniture

. . . .

The following photos are examples of furniture in the real world with descriptions of the appropriate finishes needed. The function *and* the appearance, along with the accuracy (time period appropriateness) are important to adhere to. For example, the antique replica of a Chippendale mirror (shown on page 19) should have a mellow soft shine, which it does, and not a high gloss. I hope that these photos will inspire you and help you with your finishing ideas. Whenever I look at the glow of the wood in the tiger maple and cherry blanket chest, it always makes me smile!

The closely spaced slats of this walnut Morris chair present a difficulty in applying a finish, suggesting a wipe-on finish, but the arms require protection from hard wear. A good solution is to use a wipe-on finish, built up with many coats on the arms.

Courtesy of Connecticut Valley School of Woodworking; Richard Berger, photographer

This cherry and tiger maple blanket chest is beautiful but is a challenge to finish. Oils risk blotching the cherry and yellowing the maple. A wash coat of super blond shellac will help protect the cherry from blotching before applying a wipe-on oil. A water-based topcoat will avoid yellowing the maple. The lightest wipe-on oil available (currently Minwax Wipe-On Poly) will minimize it. The design requires prefinishing the maple panels before assembly in order to minimize the risk of exposing an unfinished edge during the dry season.

This replica of a Chippendale tiger maple mirror has a sophisticated color layering scheme of stains and glazes to emphasize the figured grain and to reproduce the old maple look of a real antique. The finish can be shellac, wipe-on finish, or even aerosol lacquers. The finish is also crackled, contributing to the appearance of antiquity.

A formal dining table, such as this example in mahogany, requires a comparably formal finish that also protects the surface from occasional spills and physical wear from dishes and utensils. A rubbed-out, multi-coat film finish of traditional varnish, polyurethane, or lacquer is appropriate.

A kitchen table is used for both daily meals and occasional food preparation, requiring the most durable finish you can provide. A multi-coat film finish of traditional varnish or polyurethane will serve the purpose but may require periodic maintenance, including a new topcoat. The most durable finish is a sprayed, catalyzed lacquer.

These three items, all replicas, have quite different needs. The clock will receive minimal wear, so a shellac or wipe-on oil, rubbed out with wax, will do well. The pedestal table is a target for drinks. Use a durable polyurethane, varnish, or lacquer on the top. The base can have a wipe-on finish to match the top. The chair may receive hard daily use, depending on the household. Use a traditional varnish, polyurethane, or eight to ten wipe-on coats of a gel varnish or polyurethane.

An inlaid coffee table, such as this beautiful example, requires careful forethought. The finish should enhance the inlay, not obscure it, protect it from the possibility of a spilled drink, and have a formality consistent with the design. A brushed polyurethane, varnish, or lacquer, built up and then rubbed out, is appropriate.

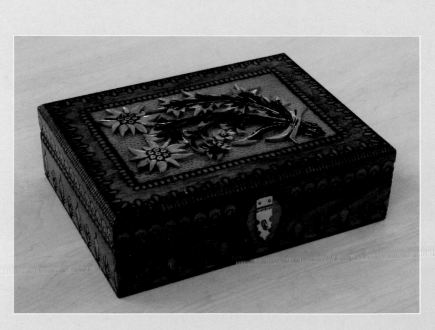

Beautifully carved and inlaid and unlikely to be abused, this jewelry box needs no more than a shellac or wipe-on product. Consider aerosols for items with carving, like this one.

A chest of drawers, such as this recently built example in cherry, requires a semi-durable topcoat to withstand daily usage but not the hard usage of dining. A wipe-on or brushed varnish or polyurethane is appropriate.

PREPARING THE WOOD

. . . .

Proper surface preparation is similar to preparing for a test. The better the preparation, the better the results. This chapter has sections that will take you step-by-step through sanding out planer marks, filling defects, conditioning the wood to take stain more evenly, and filling open pore wood to create a surface that is smoother than the actual wood itself. It also has an exercise for making a test sample such as I emphasized in Chapter 1, "Getting Started." If your surface preparation looks good in the test sample, then the same preparation will look good on your project. By the end of these exercises, you'll be able to prepare wood for the remaining finishing steps with full confidence that the wood is as ready as you're able to make it.

Smoothing the surface

By sanding through the proper sequence of grits, changing discs, and examining the surface under backlight, you build the foundation for success. The goal is a wood surface with no traces of planer marks and with sanding scratches that are too fine to be seen. The only unnatural characteristic will be its smoothness—a tree in the forest is not very smooth. For the time being we won't worry about deeper defects. We'll deal with them next.

The following tools and materials will be necessary, or at least useful, for most of the exercises in this section (see **Figure 3.1**).

Figure 3.1. The tools and materials for producing immaculately smooth wood include more than just sandpaper and a block of wood.

Tools and Materials

- Random orbit sander
- Sanding block; felt, cork, or rubber
- Bright clip-on shop light
- Shop-Vac or air compressor
- Sanding discs to fit your sander; 80 to 220 grits
- #2 pencil
- Panel or scrap of wood (hard or soft), 6" x 8"
- 9" x 11" abrasive paper; 180, 220, and 320 grit
- Tack cloth
- Denatured alcohol, lacquer thinner, or mineral spirits

Covered in this section:

Sanding
page 28

Filling Large Voids Using Epoxy Wood Dough
page 36

Filling Small Holes
page 30

Filling Large Voids Using Polyester Auto Body Filler
page 38

Matching Fillers
page 32

Filling Tearout
page 39

Filling Screw Holes
page 33

Examining Your Work
page 39

Filling Large Spider Cracks
page 34

Making Your First Step Sample
page 40

Sanding

Everyone *thinks* they know how to sand, but, in reality, not many do. For instance, do you know how long before changing to a new disc or changing into a higher grit? Do you know how fast to move the sander; do you bear down or tilt it? The answers are in this section!

Step 1: Attach a 120-grit disc to the sander; turn the tool on and gently glide the moving disc onto the surface. If the stock has come directly from a well-tuned planer or from the lumberyard, there will be evidence of "chatter marks" on the surface but not a lot of problems that are deep. The 120-grit disc is perfect for sanding until there are no traces of those marks. If there is major tearout or snipe (a gully in the wood from the planer), start with grits of 80 or 100. Give the sander time to do its job. Move it across the surface about a foot every ten seconds. Don't move it vigorously as you would a sanding block.

Step 2: With the #2 pencil, draw a random line across the surface that was sanded to 120 grit. Attach a 150-grit disc to the sander and sand off the pencil line. Apply a second pencil line and sand that off as well with the same grit. This simple procedure takes the guesswork out of changing grits (see **Figure 3.2**).

Step 3: Proceed to 180 grit in the same manner. If the panel is hardwood, 180 is adequate; stop there. If the panel is softwood, continue to 220 grit and stop.

Step 4: Cut a sheet of the same grit paper you've just been using into quarters. Wrap one of the quarters around a firm felt, rubber, or cork sanding block. Or, if you prefer, apply self-adhesive abrasive paper to the block (see **Figure 3.3**). Sand evenly and thoroughly with long, even strokes and with the grain. Always use a block when sanding flat surfaces. For curved or round surfaces, fold the quarter in thirds and sand by hand without the block (see **Figure 3.4**).

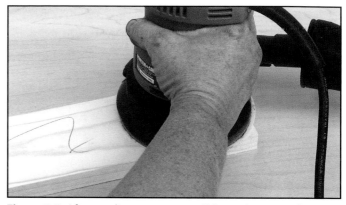

Figure 3.2. After sanding out two pencil lines, change to the next finer grit.

Figure 3.3. Self-adhesive abrasive paper on a roll is quicker and easier to use than quartered 9" x 11" sheets.

Figure 3.4. Always sand flat surfaces with the grain and with a block.

Step 5: Remove all the dust. Vacuuming up the dust is preferable because it's cleaner, but compressed air will also make quick work of it. Remove the ultra-fine dust with a tack cloth. Tack off just before the next finishing step and always after scuffing between coats. Dust removal between each grit is essential, not just to remove wood dust but to remove particles of the previous grit as well. There's no point in sanding with 150 grit if you're also pushing 120 grit around.

Step 6: Check the results with backlighting. Position a clip-on spotlight low on the end of the work surface so the light strikes the surface at a low angle. Wet the surface with any of the solvents listed in the Tools and Materials list. Immediately examine the surface, while it's still shiny wet, for problems like squiggles, crosswise scratches, low spots, glue spots, missed areas, and whatever other problems there might be. If everything looks good, lightly de-whisker the surface with the final grit, by hand. Yes, the grain does rise, even with alcohol (see **Figure 3.5**).

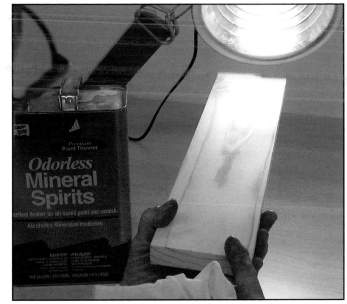

Figure 3.5. Alcohol will make "whiskers" stand up, and backlight will make them stand out.

Helpful Tip

How Long Is the Disc Effective?

Most woodworkers don't realize that efficient wood removal drops dramatically after four minutes of use. Sanding until the disc is worn down is a waste of your time. Softwoods also shorten the life of a disc by loading it up with resinous wood particles. If you are experiencing rapid wear on the outer rim of the disc, then the backup pad on your sander also needs to be replaced. The foam it is made from has swelled on the outside edge (see **Figure 3.6**).

Figure 3.6. The backup pad as well as the abrasive disc on this sander needs replacement.

Adventures in Finishing

Before continuing with this beautifully smooth panel, let me tell you another story, this time about surface prep.

One day at a restaurant, while waiting for my food, I looked down at the table's surface. The entire table was covered with long "coiled spring" marks, the dreaded pigtail squiggle (a defect created when the sander is loaded with grit and dragged around the surface). I thought to myself arrogantly, what terrible finishing! But on closer inspection I saw that there was a pattern to it. And every table in the place had the same pattern. What madman would have done this? How could one purposely create bad surface preparation? The owner had no idea who had made the tables, but he loved them. I ate, and contemplated the pigtails. This craftsman was better than me! I could never make consistent mistakes!

Filling Small Holes

Filling assembly holes from finish nails or air nailers is a necessary chore. Most woodworkers apply a big messy smear of wood filler, and, even with sanding, the area has a "halo" of filler-impregnated wood. Here is one method to avoid this problem.

Tools and Materials
- Nail set
- Painter's tape
- Small finish nail
- Wood filler

Step 1: Drive a small finish nail into a panel. Here, I'm using an oak panel. Tap it in flush (see **Figure 3.7**).

Step 2: Cover the nail with painter's tape an inch or two long (see **Figure 3.8**).

Figure 3.7. Tap the small finish nail flush into the oak panel.

Figure 3.8. Cover the nail with an inch or two of painter's tape.

Step 3: Set the nail right through the tape with the nail set (see **Figure 3.9**).

Step 4: Apply a thin smear of filler over the hole in the tape (see **Figure 3.10**).

Step 5: Let the filler dry, sand lightly with 220 grit, and then pull off the tape. The hole is nicely filled without a big, ugly mess of overfill (see **Figure 3.11**). This works well for air nailers also. Apply tape on the area just before popping off a brad, and then follow the same filling steps as above.

Figure 3.9. Set the nail right through the tape.

Figure 3.10. Apply a thin smear of filler over the hole.

Figure 3.11. Let the filler dry, sand lightly, and then pull off the tape.

Matching Fillers

This exercise takes the guesswork out of matching color, and it provides a quick and clean way to fill holes.

Tools and Materials
- Nail set or awl
- Golden oak stain
- 2-pound cut, blond, dewaxed shellac (such as Sealcoat)
- Fill stick kit

Step 1: Create some holes with a nail set or awl on a small panel. (If you've done the previous exercise, you can use the same panel.)

Step 2: Sand the panel with a block by hand because it is so small, first with 150-grit abrasive and then 180 grit. Remove the dust and tack off.

Step 3: Stain it with golden oak and let it dry as instructed on the container.

Step 4: Seal it with the shellac specified in the Tools and Materials list. Let it dry for an hour.

Step 5: From the fill stick kit, select a color that closely matches the stain on the panel (see **Figure 3.12**). Colored fill sticks are available in over a hundred colors, so close matching is usually possible. Nip off a bit of the stick with a fingernail and persuade it into the hole, slightly overfilling.

Step 6: With the heat from your hand, smooth and level the fill (see **Figure 3.13**).

Step 7: Scuff the panel with 320-grit abrasive to prepare it for the next step in the finishing process. Topcoats and sealers can be applied right over the fill stick area without problems. This method is superior to the traditional putty method because it is so clean and the color match is easier.

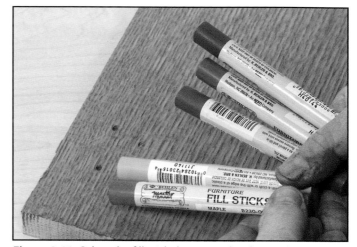

Figure 3.12. Select the fill stick that most closely matches your panel.

Figure 3.13. The warmth of your fingers is enough to soften these fillers.

Filling Screw Holes

Any hole larger than a nail head should be filled with real wood. In this exercise, we'll be using a nice wood plug set flush and sanded to perfection to create a nearly invisible patch.

Tools and Materials
- Wood screw
- Matching screw-hole bit
- Matching screw-hole plug
- Glue
- Palette knife or toothpick
- Drill with counterbore cutter

Step 1: With the proper size bit setup, complete with a counterbore cutter, drill a hole into the oak panel deep enough to allow room for the head of the screw and the plug (see **Figure 3.14**). Some bits also have a depth adjustment.

Step 2: Drive the screw in.

Step 3: Cut a plug from a scrap of the same wood as the panel, or buy face grain plugs of the correct size and species.

Step 4: Apply a small amount of glue inside the hole with a toothpick or small palette knife. Tap the plug in flush or just a tiny bit proud (see **Figure 3.15**).

Step 5: Sand the entire surface ready for finishing (see **Figure 3.16**).

Figure 3.14. Drill a hole in the panel that allows room for the screw and the plug.

Figure 3.15. Apply glue inside the hole. Do not use excessive glue! The squeeze-out will cause a mess when staining.

Figure 3.16. Sand the surface. A well-plugged hole is nearly invisible. Can you find it?

Helpful Tip _____

Abrasive Grading Systems
Some abrasives now available in this country are graded by a European grading system instead of the traditional American system. The two systems are identical up to 220 grit and then begin to diverge. The differences won't be disastrous when smoothing wood but could be quite serious when scuff sanding finishes. For details of the differences, see the sidebar Grit Grades on page 127 in Chapter 5, "Topcoating."

Filling Large Spider Cracks

Sometimes a piece of wood is so beautiful around a knot area that it's worth using in spite of the defects. Cracks from wood shrinkage can be filled with liquid two-part epoxies, which also add strength and help prevent further splitting.

Tools and Materials
- Panel with spider cracks
- Stir stick
- Duct tape
- Wax paper
- Clamp
- Liquid epoxy resin and hardener
- Dose cups
- Colorants (see Step 4)

Step 1: On the front or primary side of the wood scrap with the spider cracks, tape over the cracks with duct tape, covering a wide area (see **Figure 3.17**).

Step 2: Cover the taped area with wax paper and a flat board, and clamp the board tightly to the scrap with the cracks. This will be a dam preventing the epoxy from leaking out.

Step 3: Mix the epoxy exactly as specified by the maker! More hardener will not produce a harder epoxy. Incorrect proportions will produce a weaker epoxy. Some epoxies come with metered pumps, making it easy to get proportions right. If yours doesn't, measure carefully with dose cups, making sure you understand the marked measurements. Mix the two ingredients thoroughly with a stick, scraping the sides of the mixing container occasionally (see **Figure 3.18**).

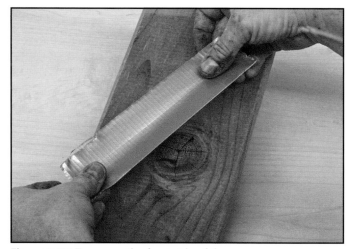

Figure 3.17. Tape over the front side of the spider cracks.

Figure 3.18. Measure liquid epoxy components precisely.

Step 4: Color the mixed epoxy. This sample will need a brown tint to blend with the surrounding knot features. You can tweak the color later with more color and graining. If colorants are not available for your brand of epoxy, use universal tinting colorants. Mix in small amounts of color until a medium tone is achieved (see **Figure 3.19**).

Step 5: With the open cracks facing up, begin pouring the epoxy into the cracks. Keep an eye on the area because the epoxy will migrate into hidden voids and will need refilling. If there are no leaks from the bottom of the board, the area will stay full when all the voids are full. Leave it slightly overfilled (see **Figure 3.20**).

Step 6: Let it cure for the manufacturer's recommended time and temperature.

Step 7: Remove the clamp, wax paper, and duct tape, and check the front, or "blind" side. It should be full and flush. If it isn't, mix a new batch with the same color and fill the voids with the blind side up this time. A dam shouldn't be necessary. Let it cure for two or three days.

Step 8: Sand both surfaces flush. After sanding, the filled area should be perfectly flush, undetectable to your fingers with your eyes closed (see **Figure 3.21**). If the color isn't quite right, it can be adjusted later in the finishing process with pigments and glazes as described on page 84.

Figure 3.19. Blend in colors to match the wood.

Figure 3.20. Filling from the back, the epoxy will migrate to the front of the board.

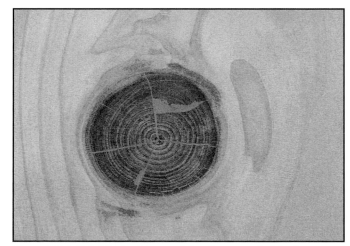

Figure 3.21. This filled spider crack has been sanded flush.

Filling Large Voids Using Epoxy Wood Dough

I strongly recommend a Dutchman—a wooden patch carefully matched to the surrounding area—for large voids, but, if the project doesn't warrant the effort involved, the following steps will produce a serviceable result using epoxy.

Tools and Materials
- Epoxy dough
- Latex gloves
- Painter's tape

Step 1: Break off a corner of or make a good-size gouge in a scrap board (see **Figure 3.22**).

Step 2: Choose a color of epoxy dough that is slightly lighter than the wood. Slice off enough of the dough to fill the hole (see **Figure 3.23**).

Step 3: Wearing gloves if your skin is sensitive, remove the plastic wrap and knead the two parts until the color is uniform (see **Figure 3.24**).

Figure 3.22. A split-off corner is a good candidate for an epoxy wood dough repair.

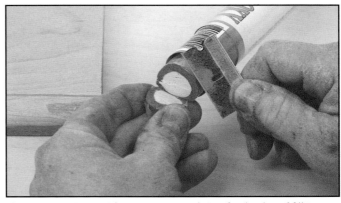

Figure 3.23. Even with experience, judging final color of fill is tricky. Aim on the lighter side. Slice off enough to fill the void.

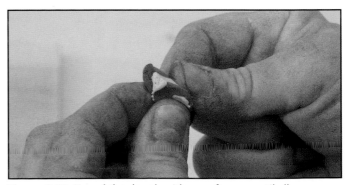

Figure 3.24. Knead the dough with your fingers until all variation in color is gone.

Step 4: Tape around the void to be filled. Allow a small space between the edge of the hole and the tape edge (see **Figure 3.25**).

Step 5: Smear the blended filler into the hole, keeping it as close to the level of the surrounding wood as possible (see **Figure 3.26**).

Step 6: Allow the epoxy to cure as instructed for the product. Some of these fillers cure in 15 minutes; others take 45 minutes.

Step 7: With a firm block and 120-grit abrasive, level the filler. If the piece is irregular, sand with folded paper and your fingers. Good painter's tape will "melt" away as you work and provides protection from such focused sanding (see **Figure 3.27**).

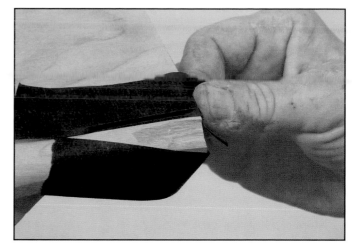

Figure 3.25. Tape off the area to be filled.

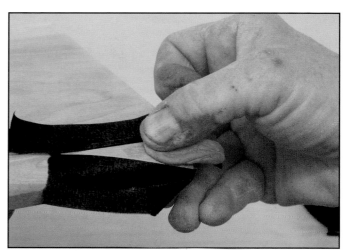

Figure 3.26. Work the blended filler firmly into the void.

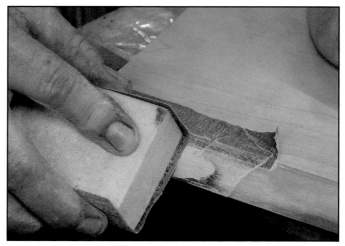

Figure 3.27. Sand the filler to a smooth continuation of the surrounding wood.

Filling Large Voids Using Polyester Auto Body Filler

Some of the best finishing products come from auto body supply stores, and polyester filler (Bondo) is one of them. It is strong, shapes well, and won't fall out like a regular wood filler. Bondo is usually white, but this exercise shows you how to color it as well as use it.

Tools and Materials
- Polyester auto body filler (such as Bondo)
- Dry pigment powders
- Palette knife
- Stir stick
- Mixing pad
- Painter's tape

Step 1: Break off a corner or make a good-size gouge in a scrap and apply tape as in the previous exercise.

Step 2: The usual mix of resin to hardener is about a golf ball-size scoop of the resin and about an inch of the hardener. Polyester fillers can be colored with dry pigment powders. Blend the pigment into the resin first, and then add the hardener and mix thoroughly with a stir stick on a mixing pad (see **Figure 3.28**).

Step 3: Smear the blended filler into the hole, keeping it as close to the level of the surrounding wood as possible (see **Figure 3.29**). Do not remove the tape.

Step 4: Allow the filler to dry hard. Polyester fillers set up fast but remain soft and gummy for an hour or more.

Step 5: With a firm block and 120-grit abrasive, level the filler (see **Figure 3.30**).

Figure 3.28. Mix resin with pigments, and then add hardener.

Figure 3.29. Apply the blended filler with a palette knife.

Figure 3.30. Smooth the cured filler to the shape of the stock.

Filling Tearout

Some defects are so tiny that fillers don't work well. CA glues are great, but they dry so fast you can't blend color into them before applying them. Here's the one-step solution.

Tools and Materials

- CA glue
- Sandpaper

Step 1: Apply drops of CA glue into the tearout spots and immediately sand the area. Dust from the sanding will blend with the glue. The sandpaper will quickly load up with the glue, so turn the paper frequently. Allow the glue to dry for an hour. This is a quick, invisible way to repair tiny defects (see **Figure 3.31**).

Figure 3.31. CA glue and sanding dust fill tiny voids, but you have to be quick.

Examining Your Work

Figure 3.32. Notice all of the irregularities. They only became apparent after applying the stain. By making a test sample, you can take steps to prevent them before staining your project.

A sanded board, with all of the visible defects filled and sanded as described in the previous exercises, can look perfect. At this point, stop and try some stain on it, and then seal and/or topcoat. You now have your first "test sample." If the result is exactly what you want your project to look like, then, as long as you treat the real project exactly as you treated the test sample, there will be no ugly surprises. The key word is "exactly." If you sand the sample more diligently or less diligently or into higher grits, apply the stain too timidly, or fuss with the sample more than is possible when finishing the project, then you are inviting surprises. In short, the test sample must reflect the process totally to achieve identical results.

If the test sample failed, producing results that you didn't anticipate (see **Figure 3.32**), study the board to find the problem areas. Scratches that you didn't notice may become highly visible when you apply stain. Or the wood may absorb more stain in some areas than others for no apparent reason. Be glad that you discovered the problems on the test sample and not on your project. The overlooked scratches are a message to sand more thoroughly and examine more carefully. The irregular absorption of stain is a message that you will need to "condition" the wood as described on page 42 before staining. This first test sample will tell you which steps to take next.

Making Your First Step Sample

As I mentioned in Chapter 1, "Getting Started," a test sample can also be elevated to what is called a step sample. This step sample will become your finishing plan. Remember to write down the details. Do not trust anything to memory, especially color! You can't possibly remember subtle shades or density of color. The step sample is your memory!

If you know what type of finish you want to use on your project, take the time now to complete a step sample. If the results are exactly what you want, you can move on to finishing your project. If the sample doesn't quite turn out the way you want, make adjustments until you get the results you're looking for. You may need to make more than one step sample.

If you're not sure what type of finish you want, browse through the chapters on coloring (page 57) and topcoating (page 91) and try some samples to find what would best suit your project. Once you've determined the products you will use, come back to this section to complete your step sample.

I'll be showing you a three-step step sample here, but be sure to adjust the procedure and materials to fit the finish you've chosen (see **Figure 3.33**).

Tools and Materials

- 4" x 18" piece of scrap from your project
- 2" chip brushes
- Painter's tape
- Any stain that you're familiar with
- 2-pound cut, blond, dewaxed shellac (such as SealCoat)
- Any topcoat that you're familiar with
- Rags
- Gloves
- Felt-tip marker (such as Sharpie)

Figure 3.33. The ingredients of a simple three-step test sample include stain, shellac, and topcoat plus the tools and materials for applying them.

Step 1: Take a piece of scrap from your project, 4" wide or so x 18" long, and sand as described on page 28.

Step 2: Stain the entire piece with your chosen stain and allow it to dry. For now, just follow the instructions on the container.

Step 3: Tape off 6" of the piece. This 6" will receive no more treatment.

Step 4: Seal the rest of the board with the shellac, and let it dry for an hour. Again, just follow the instructions on the container (see **Figure 3.34**).

Step 5: Tape off 6" of the sealed section and leave it at that.

Step 6: Topcoat the remaining section, following the instructions on the container (see **Figure 3.35**).

You now have three "steps" (see **Figure 3.36**). Remember to write the date, the client's name, and the products used on the back of the sample. This gives you a historical view of the process and illustrates how to duplicate the procedure in the future. When you are finishing your actual project, it allows you to check after each step to make sure you haven't introduced some unintended variable. When the process is a simple one, it may seem like a waste of time, but when the process is more sophisticated, with color layers for example, it is critical to document each layer.

Figure 3.34. Having stained the board and taped off 6", seal the remaining 12" with shellac.

Figure 3.35. Topcoat the last 6" of the sample.

Figure 3.36. The history of a finish: just stain at the top; stained and sealed with shellac in the middle; and stained, sealed, and topcoated at the bottom.

Controlling stain absorption

"Conditioning" is finishers' jargon for sealing wood lightly, thereby limiting the absorption of stain. Conditioners are sometimes referred to as pre-stain conditioners or stain controllers. They are important because certain woods absorb stain unevenly. The disastrous result is "blotching," uneven coloration that disrupts the beauty of the grain that we treasure (see **Figure 3.37**). Pine, cherry, maple, and sometimes birch are the woods that most frequently produce blotchy results. There is nothing more disheartening than to ruin a finely built project within a matter of minutes because of a poor staining plan. Disaster can be avoided by making a test sample using conditioners.

Tools and Materials
- 2" chip brushes
- Painter's tape
- Rags
- Jelly or pint canning jars
- Wood stir sticks
- 320-grit abrasive paper
- Tack cloth

Figure 3.38. The materials for conditioning include shellac, glue size, and denatured alcohol.

Figure 3.37. You can reduce the risk of uneven staining, as shown here, by lightly sealing the wood beforehand with a home-mixed or proprietary conditioner.

There are various off-the-shelf products labeled as stain controllers for conditioning wood, but we are going to use readily available ingredients and mix our own. The products we'll use are shellac and glue size. Other products that can achieve similar results are gel varnishes, Danish oil, and thinned versions of the actual topcoat to be used.

The following tools and materials will be necessary, or at least useful, for most of the exercises in this section (see **Figure 3.38**).

Helpful Tip

Conditioner Strength
Stronger mixes of conditioner result in lighter and more uniform color. More diluted mixes result in deeper color but have a greater risk of blotching.

Covered in this section:

Conditioning with Shellac and Glue Size
page 44

Compatibility of Conditioners with Stains
page 45

Conditioning with Gel Stain and Gel Varnish
page 46

Conditioning with Shellac and Glue Size

The woods most notorious for blotching are usually the most popular. For example, cherry is a horrible blotcher, but everyone loves to build with it. Pine is an easy wood to mill and build with, but it is a nightmare to finish. This exercise is a must if you are headed for treacherous woods!

Tools and Materials
- 18" long scrap of pine
- Pencil, pen, or marker
- 2-pound cut shellac
- Denatured alcohol
- Glue size
- Warm water
- Oil-based stain (Minwax red mahogany)

Step 1: Sand a scrap of pine about 18" long as described on page 28, and remember that pine is a softwood so sand right up to 220 grit. Vacuum off the dust and tack off as well.

Step2: Divide the board into three equal sections (across the grain) with painter's tape. Label the sections on one edge #1, #2, #3.

Step 3: Put one part 2-pound cut shellac and one part denatured alcohol together in a jar, and mix them with a stir stick. It is now approximately a 1-pound cut, and from now on we will call it our wash coat (see **Figure 3.39**). To prepare the glue size, put one part glue size and four parts warm water into another jar and stir thoroughly (see **Figure 3.40**).

Figure 3.39. One part Sealcoat plus one part alcohol equals our "wash coat."

Helpful Tip

Conditioners and Trouble Areas
Conditioners are useful for trouble areas like end grain and cross grain that suck up stain, making them very dark (see **Figure 3.41**).

Figure 3.41. The end grain on the left has been conditioned with glue size, but the end grain on the right has not.

Figure 3.40. One part full-strength glue size plus four parts warm water equals glue size conditioner.

Step 4: On section #1, do nothing. On section #2, apply an even but not flooded coat of glue size conditioner with one of the brushes (see **Figure 3.42**). On section #3, apply an even but not flooded coat of the shellac wash coat with a different brush (see **Figure 3.43**).

Step 5: Allow the conditioners to dry for 6 to 8 hours. The shellac appears to dry quickly, but the glue size is slow because of the water content.

Step 6: Lightly scuff the sections that have shellac and glue size on them with 320-grit abrasive on a block. The scuffing must be gentle because these coatings are thin. Note how smooth the surfaces are.

Step 7: Stir the oil-based stain thoroughly, and apply a generous coat across all three sections. Wait a moment and then wipe off all the excess stain. Immediately the results will be obvious (see **Figure 3.44**).

Why two kinds of conditioner? Glue size is not compatible with water-based stains, and shellac is not compatible with alcohol-based stains, as shown in the table below.

Compatibility of Conditioners with Stains

Type of Stain	Glue Size	Wash Coat of Shellac
Oil-based Stains	Yes	Yes
Water-based Stains	No	Yes
Alcohol-based Stains	Yes	No

Helpful Tip _____

Sanding Contrary Grain

Use the glue size mixture on contrary grain that is "furry," like nap on corduroy, and doesn't seem to sand off. The wood fibers stiffen up as the surface dries and sheer off nicely when sanded. Mahogany is notorious for this kind of problem. Be sure to size the entire surface to avoid a light spot.

Figure 3.42. Apply glue size to the middle section.

Figure 3.43. Apply wash coat shellac to the last section.

Figure 3.44. Notice the radical difference between the "non-conditioned" first section and the other two sections.

Conditioning with Gel Stain and Gel Varnish

In this exercise, we will use the products that you are finishing with to condition against possible blotching. This process is very easy, especially if you are a fan of gel products. Gel stains are different from other stains because they are topical. Applied to raw wood, they seldom blotch, but they can. To be safe, try them on a test sample first. We'll meet gel stains again when we get more into coloring.

Tools and Materials
- Sanded pine board, 6" x 8"
- Gel varnish
- Gel stain

Step 1: Divide a sanded pine board in half with painter's tape.

Step 2: Apply gel varnish on one half with a rag, and then remove all excess. When you're sure the excess is completely removed, allow the board to dry for eight hours.

Step 3: Gently scuff the varnished half with 320 grit. Tack off the dust.

Step 4: Apply a moderate amount of gel stain evenly, without streaks, to both halves. The result should be a consistent color on the half that had varnish first and then stain (see **Figure 3.45**).

Figure 3.45. The half on the right is lighter but has more uniform color because it received a light coat of gel varnish before staining.

Adventures in Finishing

Before we go on, let me tell you a story about someone who wanted to avoid blotching by spraying the stain instead of applying it by hand.

Yes, it was another angry call from a finisher who had been told that using a dye stain in a spray gun yields a more uniform result. (That, by the way, is true.) So this brave soul pours a red water-based dye into his gun and sets the gun for a light, fairly dry spray. Out in his informal spray booth garage, he sprays a cabinet he has built. As he sprays, the airborne dye floats onto his hair and the floor, as well as the cabinet. The white poodle comes out from the house and walks through the dye on the floor and back into the house onto the brand-new white carpet (just installed the week before) and up onto the white sofa.

Very upset, he wanted to know how to get it out of his hair, and the dog's, and how to remove the paw prints from the white rug, and the sofa!

After a moment to suppress a giggle, my first advice was to get a haircut.

Adventures in Finishing

Remember to always read the manufacturer's directions with any finishing product. Some don't read instructions, like the man in this story:

I wish he hadn't called. He was irate and looking for someone other than himself to blame. After calming him down, I got the details. He had chosen a two part epoxy for a floor finish because of its water resistance and durability. He had applied it over two weeks before and only parts of it were dry. In other places it was still gooey. When I asked how he applied it, he angrily shouted that he had carefully brushed on Part A, then Part B! I quietly told him that the directions said to thoroughly mix part A and part B and to apply the mixture. There was dead silence on the other end; he hadn't read the directions. When he grudgingly asked how he could get this partially cured, partially gooey "molasses" off the floor I said something about a shovel, and then I heard a click.

Filling the grain

Filling the tiny natural voids in open-grained woods with a silica-based material is called grain or pore filling. The most common open-grained woods are oak, walnut, ash, mahogany, and rosewood. There are many others. Grain can also be filled with finish but doing so is much more difficult and time consuming than using grain fillers, and the grain is likely to reappear as the finish ages and shrinks.

Years ago, grain was filled with plaster of Paris (a form of silica) colored with pigments. The materials used in modern oil-based fillers are a finer-grain silica suspended in oil, solvents, driers, and pigment colorants. They allow a comfortable open time and allow you to stain before filling. The exercises that follow explore that in more detail.

As you can see in **Figure 3.46**, the tools for filling grain are not high tech. The burlap and the plastic scrapers are ordinary items, but they work the best. Trust me—there is no better way to remove this grain-filling mud!

There are three reasons for grain filling; the first is functional. The grain filler smoothes surfaces such as oak or mahogany on a desk surface to keep a penpoint from falling into the grain "pits." A desk blotter does the same thing, but some people prefer a blotter-free wood surface.

The second reason for grain filling is decorative; grain filler can dramatize the grain. Oak, for example, can be colored with a black dye and then the pores filled with a white filler (see **Figure 3.47**). Mica powders can also be added to grain fillers to create gold, copper, silver, or many other "sparkle" effects in the grain (see **Figure 3.48**).

And third, filling the grain is the initial step in a piano, or formal, finish. These are glasslike surfaces with no visible grain texture of any sort. A formal mahogany dining room table is a good example. They are sophisticated, time-consuming finishes. Filling the grain is only the first of many steps including sealing, glazing, sealing again, and then applying seven to ten layers of topcoat. Finally, it all has to be cured and polished out (see **Figure 3.49**). Whew!

Tools and Materials

- Plastic scrapers or old credit cards
- 2" chip brushes
- 12" x 12" squares of burlap
- Stir sticks
- Mineral spirits
- Jars with lids, or cups
- Rags
- Fine abrasive pads (such as Scotchbrite)
- Measuring cups and spoons

Helpful Tip _____

Water-Based Grain Fillers

Though not covered in this book, there are water-based grain fillers on the market as well. One of them uses silica like its oil-based counterpart, but its base is water rather than oil. These products dry rapidly and are meant to be put on, allowed to dry, and then sanded back. Staining first, before grain filling, with a water-based product is difficult. The other water-based filler is transparent, with no particles. It's a heavy-bodied, gel-like material that is spread on, removed quickly and cleanly, and sanded lightly to clean up the surface. It is truly transparent and does little in coloring the wood or the pores. It dries fast, so be careful. If you decide to use either of these products, follow the directions closely.

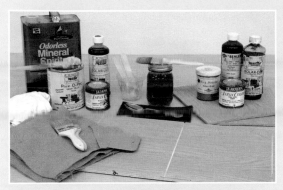

Figure 3.46. Like most finishing processes, grain filling involves proprietary products and solvents. Unlike others, it requires removing product from the surface while leaving it in the tiny pores of the wood, hence the scrapers and burlap.

Figure 3.47. By using colored grain fillers, you can color the wood in a way that adds decorative color while emphasizing the grain rather than covering it up.

Figure 3.48. Adding mica to grain filler adds a sparkle as well as color.

Figure 3.49. A piano finish is the culmination of many finishing skills, achieving a glasslike surface on beautiful woods.

Covered in this section:

Making a Four-Part Test Board with Conventional Grain Filler
page 50

Filling Grain Using Mica
page 54

Filling Grain with Contrasting Colors
page 55

Making a Four-Part Test Board with Conventional Grain Filler

If grain filling is a completely new experience, this exercise will demystify the whole process. We'll be making a four-part panel that will answer all the ways wood grain can be filled.

> **Tools and Materials**
> - Oak plywood, 12" wide x 36" long
> - Wash coat
> - Golden oak or similar dye-based non-grain-raising stain (such as Solar-Lux)
> - Grain filler, oil based, such as Behlen's Pore-O-Pac
> - Burnt umber Japan color
> - Mineral spirits

Step 1: Divide the oak plywood across the grain into four 9" sections with saw kerfs. (Kerfs will prevent the dye from wicking into adjoining sections.)

Step 2: Sand the oak plywood carefully. The top veneer is extremely thin, so the risk of sanding through is high. Plywood is factory sanded with abrasives in the 120- to 150-grit range, so begin sanding with 150 grit. Use the pencil line method described on page 28. Vacuum, apply a pencil line, and sand off the line with 180 grit. Then, block sand lightly with 180 grit.

Step 3: Label the four sections #1, #2, #3, and #4 along an edge.

Step 4: Do nothing to square #1. Apply an even but not flooded wash coat to Square #2 (see **Figure 3.50**).

Step 5: Stain squares #3 and #4 with the non-grain-raising dye stain. This is an alcohol-based product and can be applied with a rag or by brush (see **Figure 3.51**). Applying by brush will lay down a heavier coat. With either method, work quickly and wipe off quickly. If the dye is uneven, you can manipulate it with a cloth dampened with water. Simply stroke lightly in the direction of the grain until the color looks more consistent.

Step 6: Allow it to dry for 6 to 8 hours.

Figure 3.50. Apply an even wash coat to Square #2. Be careful on multi-step test samples so you don't dribble on adjoining sections.

Figure 3.51. Applying stain by rag allows more control on a small surface than applying by brush.

Step 7: Apply a wash coat to section #4 by brush. Work quickly and apply the wash coat in one direction only. Do not overbrush; leave it alone once applied or use an aerosol shellac (see **Figure 3.52**).

Step 8: Allow the wash coat to dry for 1 to 3 hours.

Step 9: Mix the grain filler thoroughly. This product has the consistency of cold peanut butter. Stir and stir and stir some more. Spoon or scoop about a ½ cup into a jar or mixing cup. Add a tablespoon of burnt umber Japan color to the filler and mix it in (see **Figure 3.53**). Thin the mixture with mineral spirits (or naphtha, which dries faster) to a consistency of heavy cream.

Step 10: Brush the creamy filler mixture across all four sections in a heavy wet film without puddles. Allow the filler to "haze up" or become dull (similar to the way car wax hazes over).

Step 11: Draw a plastic scraper diagonally across the grain, pulling off all of the heaviest residue (see **Figure 3.54**).

Figure 3.52. When applying a shellac over an alcohol-based stain, lay it down and leave it alone so you don't pick up the color.

Figure 3.53. Adding Japan color to grain filler is the fastest way to impact the color of the filler and aids in drying.

Figure 3.54. When scraping off excess grain filler, work in a direction that cleans the surface but leaves the pores full of filler.

Step 12: Clean off any filler remaining on the surface with burlap. Rub lightly in small circles, turning the burlap often, and when it's mostly streak free, wipe with the grain. The goal is a clean, streak-free surface with no ridges or swirls of grain filler on the "upper wood" (see **Figure 3.55**). Allow it to dry for 6 to 8 hours.

Step 13: When the filler is dry, the surface will still have minute particles or crumbs on it. Smooth it off with an abrasive pad, also removing any discrepancies missed in Step 12. If the wood is very grainy, you may need to fill it again. Now is the time to do so by starting again with Step 9.

Step 14: The final step is a light, even wash coat. Let it dry before continuing with more color or topcoating.

Step 15: Prop up the panel and step back. It will tell the story. In fact, it's a "storyboard" (see **Figure 3.56**). Since results will vary with different species of wood and different colors of stain and filler, test samples are essential. The board shows all of the ways that wood grain can be filled with an oil-based filler. There is no wrong or right way. As a finisher, you must decide which way produces the result that you want for the project at hand.

Figure 3.55. Grain filler should remain in the pores but not on the surface.

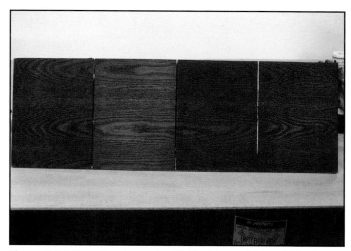

Figure 3.56. Wood grain can be filled with an oil-based filler in four ways, from left to right: on raw wood, on a wash coat, after stain, and after stain and wash coat.

Notice however:

On Square # 1: With neither stain nor wash coat, the colorant in the filler also colored the raw wood.

On Square #2: The wash coat kept the upper wood cleaner and brighter. It was also easier to remove the excess.

On Square #3: Because the square was stained but not wash coated, the colorant in the filler changed the stain color.

On Square #4: Because this square was stained and then wash coated, it is not only the brightest but also the most work.

Helpful Tip _____

Choosing Grain Filler Color
Decide on the color of the grain filler early in the design of the finish. Few grain fillers accept stain when fully dry, so color is very difficult to change after the grain is filled.

Filling Grain Using Mica

These abbreviated instructions assume that you have completed the previous exercise, Making a Four-Part Test Board with Conventional Grain Filler. If you haven't, I strongly urge you to complete that exercise before tackling this one.

Tools and Materials

- Oak panel
- 320-grit sandpaper and sanding block
- Mica powder (Aztec gold is my favorite, but you choose)
- Bright red non-grain-raising stain

Step 1: Prepare an oak panel, vacuum, and then tack off.

Step 2: Stain, if desired, or simply wash coat. Allow it to dry and scuff gently with 320 grit on a block.

Step 3: Scoop a ½ cup of grain filler into a jar or cup. Add 2 tablespoons of mica powder to the filler and mix well. Thin the material with mineral spirits to the consistency of heavy cream (see **Figure 3.57**).

Step 4: Apply the filler to the oak panel, keeping the upper wood as clean and free of gold contaminant as possible. Allow it to dry; then scrub off any crumbs with an abrasive pad.

Step 5: Apply a topcoating. A glossy coating will bring out the sparkle more than a flat or satin coating (see **Figure 3.58**).

Figure 3.57. Two tablespoons of mica powder in a half-cup of filler gives good sparkle.

Figure 3.58. A glossy topcoat brings out the sparkle more.

Filling Grain with Contrasting Colors

This brief exercise will take you through the steps that produced the black and white finished board shown at the beginning of this section, Filling the Grain, found on page 49, **Figure 3.47**).

As in the previous exercise, these abbreviated instructions assume that you have completed the step-by-step exercise Making a Four-Part Test Board with Conventional Grain Filler on page 50. If you haven't, I strongly urge you to complete that exercise before tackling this one.

Step 1: Prepare an oak panel, vacuum, then tack off.

Step 2: Apply the black non-grain-raising dye stain with a rag or a brush; work "wet and fast." Even out any unevenness with a water-dampened cloth. Allow it to dry for 3 to 4 hours.

Step 3: Wash coat the black surface, and remember to work quickly in one direction. Do not overbrush. You can use an aerosol shellac instead. Scuff lightly with 320 grit on a block.

Step 4: Thoroughly mix a ½ cup of grain filler with a tablespoon of white Japan color. Thin to heavy cream consistency.

Step 5: Apply the white grain filler, scrape, and scrub with burlap, making sure the upper wood is cleaned of any white haze (see **Figure 3.59**). Allow it to dry, and scrub off any crumbs with an abrasive pad.

Step 6: Topcoat with any product.

Tools and Materials

- Oak panel
- 320-grit sandpaper and sanding block
- Jet black non-grain-raising dye stain
- Grain filler (oil based)
- White Japan color

Figure 3.59. Your first hint of the final result comes when you begin scraping off the excess filler.

Adventures in Finishing

And now, a grain filling story.

I'll never think of grain filling again without going back to 9/11. I was teaching in Maine, describing the process of filling the pores. The director of the school rushed in and announced that something was going down in New York. At first we all thought it was a joke, but his face wasn't saying so. All of my students scattered to phones and cell phones. It wasn't until after lunch that almost everyone reappeared, somewhat relieved about their families and situations. Only one student had to leave because he and his family lived near the zone.

As we sat at our benches, I wondered what possible significance grain filling could have. However, we did pick up where we left off, and the afternoon was spent in innocent work on our test samples. One student mentioned later that it was a welcome respite, for a short while, when everything else was just too much.

CHAPTER 4

COLORING WOOD

Coloring wood has great potential for beautiful, creative results—and for unhappy surprises. After completing the step-by-step exercises in this chapter, you'll be able to create the beautiful results with little risk of disappointment. The exercises explore the wide variety of stains on the market and how to use them.

The variety can be bewildering, and choosing can be confusing, but grouping products into broad categories based on final visual impact narrows down the choices. Begin with the difference in appearance between pigment stains and dye stains. Pigment stains are muted and less vivid. Dye stains are very transparent and bright. They permeate the cellulose of the wood, highlighting the natural grain figure. One is not better than the other; they are just different. Each has its place, and the wood finisher must choose which is more appropriate for the project at hand.

The pigment vs. dye distinction among stains, while important, is only one of several ways that the many stains on the market can be categorized. Other distinctions include the solvent or carrier used, the physical form of the product such as liquid or gel, and the presence or absence of special additives such as driers. Since this book is intended primarily as a guide for woodworkers in becoming familiar with the working characteristics of the many choices available, I have chosen to group products in a way that has proven helpful in the classes and seminars that I teach.

There are many products listed in the exercises that follow. These are not all of the stains on the market, nor do you need to purchase all of the ones listed. I do suggest that you read through the exercises within a category before selecting the ones that most interest you, and then follow the appropriate exercises to produce your own test samples. We'll work first with pigment stains.

Pigment stains

Most pigment stains are easy to use. Remember that these stains tend to obscure the wood more than dye stains, but they don't fade as much as dye stains do. The pigments are typically carried by oil, sometimes by water, and are applied by flooding the surface and then wiping off the excess (see **Figure 4.1**). They are relatively "lazy" stains because the dry time is long and there is no rush when working with them.

Pigment stains (see **Figure 4.2**) that use oil as their "base" have been around a long time and are quite commonly available. The oil "carries" the pigments making it easy to spread the pigments evenly on the wood. After the excess is wiped off, the product is allowed to cure, or dry. As it does so, the oil bonds to the wood, binds the pigments to the wood, and forms a thin film on the surface of the wood.

Manufacturers have learned to adjust the behavior of these basic stains by careful selection of the particular oils that they use and by adding other ingredients, almost always including solvents that evaporate as one part of the drying or curing process. One result of careful selection of oils and solvents is an oil-based pigment stain that dries or cures fairly quickly, allowing the user to proceed to the next stage of finishing with less wait. These stains are called quick-drying or fast-drying or are given a trade name that conveys that idea.

Another modification of the basic oil-and-pigment recipe is a proportion of pigment to oil that favors the oil and decreases the pigment. Together with careful selection of the oils used, the result is a product that builds a heavier film on the surface of the wood without obscuring the wood with too much pigment. These popular products are commonly known as Danish oils or colored oils. Note that they differ from traditional oil stains by their proportions and purpose more than by any fundamental difference in ingredients.

Tools and Materials

- Panel or scrap of wood (hard or soft), 6" x 8"
- 2" chip brushes
- Sponges
- Felt sanding block
- Stir sticks
- Cups and jars
- Mixing containers
- Dose cups
- Rags
- Disposable gloves
- Fine paint filters
- Fine abrasive pads (such as Scotchbrite)
- 220-grit abrasive paper

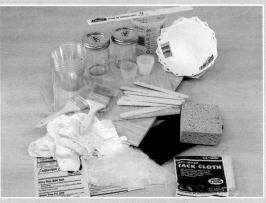

Figure 4.1. Shown here are the basic tools for measuring, mixing, and using stains.

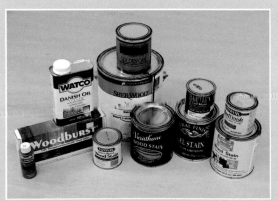

Figure 4.2. These are just a few pigment-based stains out of the dozens and dozens on the market.

A third popular modification, found in gel stains, changes the flow characteristics of the product so that it tends to remain on the surface of the wood rather than soak in. This is useful with woods that have uneven absorbency, tending to soak up more stain in some areas and less in others, giving a blotchy appearance. It also helps control the product when applying it to non-horizontal surfaces. If you haven't used gel stains, you're in for some pleasant surprises. They behave somewhat like mayonnaise, allowing you to easily spread them around, but they don't drip and flow on their own. (For the technically inclined, they are thixotropic.)

The last variation among pigment stains departs from the oil-and-pigment formulation by using water with various additives instead of oil to carry the pigment and to bind it to the wood. They have the environmental advantage of minimizing volatile organic compounds (VOCs) and the convenience of water cleanup.

Covered in this section:

Applying Oil-Based Pigment Wiping Stains

Applying Quick-Dry Wiping Stains

Applying Colored Oils

Applying Gel Pigment Stains

Applying Water-Based Pigment Stains

Applying Oil-Based Pigment Wiping Stains

These are the most common stains found in local hardware and home improvement stores. While they may have dyes in them as well as pigments, they rely mostly on pigment for color, leaving the soft, muted characteristics of pigment stains. Relatively easy to use, they provide the consumer with predictable results with two exceptions: They have a tendency to give blotchy results as described in Chapter 3 on page 42, and they tend to "weep" out of the grain on woods like oak as described in **Figure 4.4.**

> **Tools and Materials**
> - Golden oak oil-based pigment wiping stain (such as Varathane Wood Stain or Minwax Wood Finish)

Step 1: Ventilate the work area well. The solvents in these stains are mineral spirits and can affect those who are sensitive.

Step 2: Open the can and stir the contents well. The pigment will be a sludge at the bottom of the can and needs to come up to the top and blend with the liquid.

Step 3: Apply the stain with a chip brush. Flow the stain on wet but not in puddles. Wait a few moments and wipe off all excess cleanly (see **Figure 4.3**).

Step 4: Take care of the oil-soaked rags immediately! The oily rag container is the official way to take care of this hazard, but other methods are described in the Safety section of Chapter 1 on page 12.

Step 5: Check regularly during the first couple of hours of drying and wipe off any "weeping" of stain from the pores (see Figure 4.4). Dry time is usually 6 to 8 hours before continuing with more finishing steps.

Figure 4.3. Flow the stain on, let it soak in, and wipe off the excess.

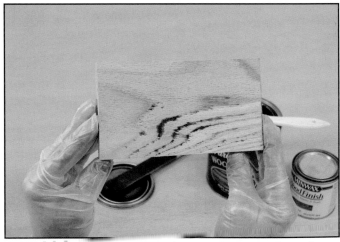

Figure 4.4. Stain can weep from the pores for over an hour after wiping off the excess. Watch for it and wipe it off because, if it dries, it will be a chore to clean up.

Applying Quick-Dry Wiping Stains

Quick-dry wiping stains are similar in many ways to the oil-based pigment wiping stains of the previous exercise but also differ in significant ways. The obvious difference is that they dry more quickly. The rapid drying then has significant positive consequences including less (but not zero) tendency to blotch and virtually no tendency to weep out of the pores of woods like oak. The rapid drying, reduced tendency to blotch, and elimination of weeping are all welcome differences. Less welcome is the powerful odor of the solvents that help them dry quickly—they can be overwhelming, and serious ventilation is necessary. Application is identical: flood the wood, let it soak in a bit, and wipe off the excess.

Tools and Materials

- Quick dry wiping stains (such as Behlen Master 15-Minute Pigmented Wood Stain or Sherwin Williams Wiping Stain in Golden Oak colors) (see **Figure 4.5**)

Step 1: Ventilate the area well before using these quick-dry stains. The solvents in them are more powerful than mineral spirits.

Step 2: Open the can and stir the contents well.

Step 3: Apply the stain with a chip brush. Flow the stain on wet but not in puddles. Wait a few moments and wipe off all excess cleanly (see Figure 4.5). Dry time is usually 15 to 30 minutes before topcoating.

Figure 4.5. Wipe off any excess cleanly. You can adjust the color of quick-dry wiping stains with up to 20% of Chroma-Chem 844 Colorants or Behlen Master Color.

Applying Colored Oils

These are the very popular "Danish" or "wiping" oils with color added. Many are also available "natural," meaning that they are oil finishes without any added color. They have a natural-wood appearance and are very easy to use. As a final finish, they offer some protection against soiling but virtually none against physical abuse. On the other hand, if they are damaged, they are much easier to restore to their original appearance than is a sophisticated, multi-layer finish. Problems in using colored oils are the same as with all slow-drying oil stains; they tend to bleed from the open pores of many woods, particularly oak, until they are fully dry, and they tend to produce a blotchy appearance on woods that absorb oils unevenly, particularly pine.

> **Tools and Materials**
> - Colored oils (such as Woodburst Woodtone Kit, colonial oak, or Watco Danish oil, golden oak)

Step 1: Thoroughly mix the colored oil product you have chosen by vigorously shaking the container.

Step 2: Pour a small puddle of the product onto a panel, and spread it over the entire panel with a rag or brush (see **Figure 4.6**). Allow the wood to absorb it for a few minutes, and then wipe off the excess.

Step 3: Take care of the oil-soaked rags immediately! The oily rag container is the official way to take care of this hazard, but other methods are described on page 14.

Step 4: Check every 15 minutes or so for any tendency of the oils to bleed out of the pores. They will wait until you aren't looking and "pop" back out of the grain—especially with oak. Wipe the oil "pops" off each time. Dry time is usually overnight. Allowed to cure on the surface, the "pops" become glossy spots, and your only recourse is to abrade them off with an abrasive pad lubricated with plenty of the same oil (see **Figure 4.7**).

Figure 4.6. Application at its easiest: pour it on, spread it around, let it soak, and wipe it off.

Figure 4.7. Bleeding wood is not pretty. Watch like a hawk and wipe it off.

Applying Gel Pigment Stains

Gel stains are ideal for woods that tend to accept stain unevenly because of variations in the absorbency of the wood—pine being the most notorious culprit. The gel structure of the product limits absorption regardless of the native absorbency of the wood. On the other hand, the limited absorption may prevent development of deep color with a single application. Gel stains are also very handy for applying stain to surfaces that cannot be laid flat; the consistency of the product prevents it from running down in streaks.

Tools and Materials

- Gel pigment stain (such as General Finishes Gel Stain or Bartley Gel Stain in Golden Oak colors)

Step 1: Open the can of gel stain and notice the jellylike consistency (see **Figure 4.8**). It isn't necessary to stir these products. Stirring reduces the gel to liquid; then you will have to let it sit still so it can return to a gel.

Step 2: Apply the stain evenly with a chip brush or rag. Work the surface with a clean rag until the color is even and has no streaks or heavy spots (see **Figure 4.9**).

Step 3: Allow it to dry, usually 6 hours. The color will be pale because gels remain on the surface. Reapply for greater color but beware of murky results from too many layers.

Figure 4.8. Note the consistency; gel stains don't flow.

Figure 4.9. Gel stains spread easily with either brush or rag. Work the surface until it has neither streaks nor heavy spots.

Applying Water-Based Pigment Stains

Finishing products that rely on water as the solvent or carrier for other ingredients are a recent technological innovation, still evolving and getting better all the time. Like the oil-based products that they are intended to replace, they have both advantages and disadvantages. One of their main advantages in the grand scheme of things is the elimination of volatile organic compounds (VOCs) from the products. Considering the enormous volume of finishing products used in industry, the elimination of VOCs is quite significant for the environment. On the personal level, water vapor is much safer to breathe than, say, mineral spirits fumes. This toxicity advantage extends to cleanup as well as to actual product application.

A second significant advantage of water over oils and mineral spirits is fire safety. When stains are applied generously and then the excess is wiped off with rags, the inevitable result is a pile of product-soaked rags. Oil-soaked rags are notorious for spontaneously bursting into flame and igniting factories, shops, garages, houses, etc. Water-soaked rags don't.

Then, there's the flip-side of the coin: water raises grain. Dampen the immaculately smooth surface of a meticulously sanded board, allow the moisture to evaporate, and run your fingertips over what now feels like a bad five-o'clock shadow. Water-based products require an entire step not required by oil-based products: "dewhiskering."

Tools and Materials
- Water-based pigment stain (such as Minwax Water-Based Wood Stain or General Finishes EF Water-Based Wood Stain in Golden Oak colors)
- 220-grit abrasive

Helpful Tip ───────

Variations in Drying Times
Dry time varies. Even if the instructions on the can say 8 hours, drying depends on your particular environment. Oil-based products dry much more slowly if it's cold or humid. Test how it feels and how it scuff sands. If it feels gummy, definitely wait longer. If you begin scuffing with 220 or 320 and the paper grabs or it loads up with finish, wait longer.

Figure 4.10. A wipe with water raises the grain.

Step 1: Raise the grain on the panel by wiping it with a water-dampened rag (see **Figure 4.10**).

Step 2: Allow it to dry for an hour or so; then, "dewhisker" it by gently hand sanding with a block and 220-grit abrasive. This process greatly reduces the amount of grain raising that might occur when you apply the water-based stain.

Step 3: Stir the stain to blend in the sludge at the bottom.

Step 4: Apply the stain with either a brush or a rag, and then wipe off the excess with a clean rag. Dry time is 3 to 4 hours between coats of stain (if a deeper shade is desired) and 8 hours before topcoating with the finish of your choice.

Dye stains

Dye stains color wood without masking the grain as much as pigment stains do. There may be minor exceptions to that rule, but as a general rule it tells the story. Use them for bright, transparent effects.

Two types of dye stain are in common use: those that dissolve in water and those that dissolve in alcohol. The latter are commonly called non-grain-raising (NGR) stains. Water-based dyes can be applied with a rag, sponge, brush, spray gun, or plant mister. Straight non-grain-raising dyes are best applied with a spray gun because they dry so quickly, but you can slow them down with a retarder for hand application with a rag, brush, or sponge (see **Figure 4.11**). Depending on the project and how complicated it is (corners, cracks, and crevices), you may need all three to get the stain spread around. Big, flat surfaces are stained more easily by rag or sponge.

Tools and Materials

- Panel or scrap of wood (hard or soft), 6" x 8"
- Sponge
- Sanding block
- 220-grit abrasive
- Postal scale
- Rags
- Chip brush
- Gloves

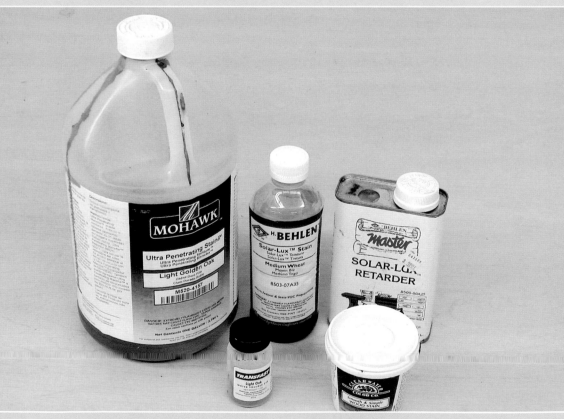

Figure 4.11. In addition to the tools listed, you'll need products for the specific exercises.

Covered in this section:

Applying Water-Soluble Aniline Dye

Conventional wisdom holds that water-soluble dyes are the best to use. The water evaporates slowly enough that the dye doesn't "get ahead of you," and lap marks are easily removed with a damp cloth. They also soak more deeply into the wood than non-grain-raising dyes. On the other hand, they fade more easily in sunlight.

Tools and Materials
- Water-soluble aniline dye in Light Golden Oak (such as Transfast Water-Soluble Dye)
- Distilled water or warm water

Step 1: Prepare a panel as described on page 28. Make sure all the dust is thoroughly removed.

Step 2: Wipe the panel with a water-dampened sponge across the grain. Allow the wood to dry; then, gently hand sand with a block and 220-grit abrasive. This raises the grain and cuts it off so it won't raise as severely when the water-based aniline dye is applied.

Step 3: These dyes are bought as powders and are then mixed in very warm but not boiling water. Distilled water is best but not essential. Follow the proportion of powder to water recommended on the container. The proportion varies from brand to brand. A postal scale is a handy way to measure small quantities of powder. For very small quantities, use a lab or pharmaceutical balance. The mix for the powdered dye in the photo is 1 ounce of powder to 2 quarts of water (the small container of dye shown holds 1 ounce) (see **Figure 4.12**). For smaller amounts, reduce both components by the same proportion. If a stronger stain is desired, the amount of powder can always be increased. Mix well, allow to cool, and then strain through a fine paint filter. Keep a record of your mixture amounts. The more accurately you measure, the more useful your records will be.

Step 4: Apply the dye with a rag, sponge, or brush (see **Figure 4.13**). Do not let it sit. Wipe off any excess. (Gloves are highly recommended because of the permanence of the color on your skin.) Work quickly and try to avoid "stop and start" marks in the middle of the panel. If lap marks occur, stroke them with a water-dampened rag until the color evens out. Wait at least 8 hours before any more finishing.

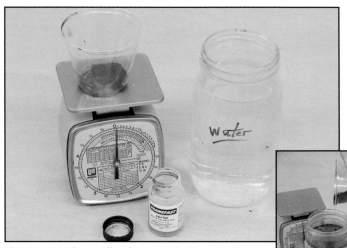

Figure 4.12. The smaller the quantity, the more important the scale. Here, a half-bottle of dye (1 ounce) will be mixed with a quart of water, and you might be able to eyeball it. But if you only need a pint, measuring a half-ounce of dye requires an accurate scale.

Figure 4.13. Apply water-soluble dyes with whatever works best for you: rag, sponge, or brush.

Helpful Tip

Sealing with Wash Coats

These stains, even when dry, can be picked up with a brush full of the sealer or topcoat that comes next (see **Figure 4.14**). This is especially true if the next coat is a water-based product. To prevent color "pull" or "bleed up," seal the dye with a wash coat.

Figure 4.14. Note the stained brush. The water-based topcoat has picked up the water-soluble dye from the board.

Helpful Tip

Removing Dye from Skin

Dyes are tough to get out of skin, but there are hand cleaners that will do it. Reduran actually removes dye, and the other product, Cupran, will remove paint. See Product Sources on page 188 for where to get them (see **Figure 4.15**).

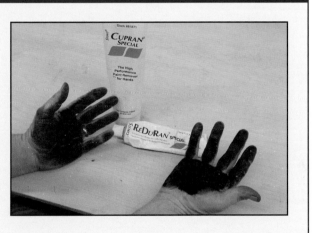

Figure 4.15. The products shown will remove dye. Latex gloves would have kept the hands clean.

Applying Non-Grain-Raising Dyes by Hand

The non-grain-raising, alcohol-soluble dyes were designed for spraying by advanced finishers in a spray room. Spraying these dyes rather than applying them by hand does indeed make a difference. Control is more precise. But with care they can be applied by hand, providing more light resistance and raising the grain less than other types of dyes. The retarder (see Tools and Materials list at right) is essential for hand application to slow the evaporation.

Tools and Materials

- Non-grain-raising stains (such as Behlen Solar-Lux medium wheat or Mohawk light golden oak)
- Retarder (such as Solar-Lux)

Step 1: Alcohol doesn't raise grain, but it readily absorbs moisture from the atmosphere, and that moisture can raise the grain. If you want to be thorough, and cautious, dampen the wood, let it dry, and then gently hand sand with a block and 220-grit abrasive.

Step 2: Prepare the stain with the retarder by stirring in one part retarder to ten parts stain. Prepare an amount that allows you to easily measure both components (see **Figure 4.16**). (Stirring straight non-grain-raising dyes is not necessary since none of the ingredients settle to the bottom.)

Step 3: Apply the stain quickly; work wet and fast. Any inconsistencies of color or lap marks can be corrected with a water-dampened rag. Dry time is 6 to 8 hours. The retarder slows the drying somewhat.

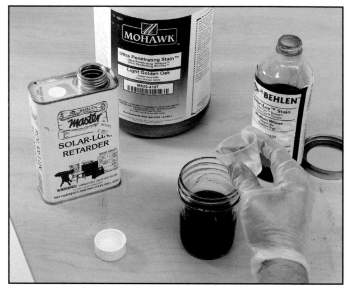

Figure 4.16. Mix one part retarder with ten parts non-grain-raising stain to slow it down enough for hand application.

Helpful Tip

Shellac and Non-Grain-Raising Stains

Because non-grain-raising stains are alcohol based, a shellac wash coat will pick up some of the color. Work with the brush full of shellac, quickly, and in one direction. Do not overbrush. You can avoid the risks of brushing shellac over non-grain-raising stains by using an aerosol shellac applied thinly or by sealing with Danish oil, which contains no alcohol. Check the final result with a test sample before committing your project to any material, sequence of materials, or procedure.

Applying Water-Based Gel Stains

These products contain water-soluble dyes and have a jellylike consistency like their oil-based counterparts; they are not meant to be stirred. They are easier to use than the non-grain-raising dyes, and, being topical, they are very useful on blotch-prone woods.

Tools and Materials
- Water-based gel stain, golden oak (such as Clearwater Color)

Step 1: Apply the gel stain with a rag, brush, or fine abrasive pad (see **Figure 4.17**). Remove the excess immediately by wiping with a rag. Dry time is long, 8 hours, because of the water base.

Step 2: Apply a wash coat of shellac or an oil-based sealer to prevent color lift before moving on to the next step in your finishing plan.

Figure 4.17. An abrasive pad works well for applying gel products.

Helpful Tip

Raising the Grain
Water-based gel stains raise grain also. Raise the grain and sand it back as in Step 1 on page 65.

Mixing wood colorants from concentrates

Concentrated wood colorants are the actual color ingredients of paints, stains, and other color products used in finishing wood. The primary colorants are pigments and dyes although, as you will see later on in the book, other colorants are also used, particularly minerals or "earths" as used in milk paint. The pigments and dyes are readily available to wood finishers in a wide variety of colors and are useful for tweaking the color of stains and glazes that are almost the right color for your application (see **Figure 4.18**). They can also be used to make your own stain, which is a good way to become familiar with them.

When working with concentrated colorants, you will need the items on the Tools and Materials list below, in addition to the actual products for the specific exercises.

Figure 4.18. These are the concentrates we will be working with in this section. Note the appropriate solvents behind them.

Tools and Materials
- Small mixing cups
- Rags
- Chip brushes
- Panel or scrap of wood (hard or soft), 6" x 8"
- Measuring cups and spoons

Covered in this section:

Using Concentrated Dyes

page 71

Using Japan Colors

page 76

Using Base Tints

page 77

Using Concentrated Dyes

These dye colors are extremely concentrated. They are packaged in handy dropper bottles for convenient measurement. Keep track of the formula when mixing your own stains; in this case, count the drops used in a specific volume of finish. These dyes can be used to tint products such as shellac, lacquer, alcohol-based stains (non-grain-raising stains), and water-based products. They can also be used in water or alcohol to make stains, as follows.

> **Tools and Materials**
> - Concentrated dyes (such as TransTints or Wizard Tints)
> - Denatured alcohol (optional)
> - Retarder (such as Solar-Lux Retarder) (optional)
> - Mixing jar

Step 1: Pour a small measured amount of water or denatured alcohol into a cup. Drop by drop, add dye concentrate until it appears to have good color density (see **Figure 4.19**). Try it on a scrap. Keep mixing until you achieve the color and color density that you want. Pour the mix into a covered jar to prevent evaporation. The retarder used in the Apply Non-Grain-Raising Dyes by Hand section (page 70) can be used if you're mixing dye with alcohol. Maintain the 10% dilution ratio.

Step 2: Apply this dye in the same manner as the water-based aniline or alcohol non-grain-raising stains—wet and fast. If necessary, smooth out any lap marks or heavy spots with a water-dampened rag. Dry time is 8 hours.

Step 3: Apply a wash coat of shellac, brushed or aerosol, or a thin coat of Danish oil to set the dye color and prevent color lift.

Figure 4.19. Count the drops as you add dye concentrate to a measured amount of solvent; then note what you used so you can reproduce the same results.

Adventures in Finishing

A test sample is so important, especially when working with color. Here's a story about a time when a test sample would have saved a lot of heartache.

I was just fourteen and tired of public schools. I wanted to be a day student at a private school in the next town over. My family wasn't rich, and my mom told me that if I wanted to go, I had to earn some of the money. Well, being fourteen, I was an expert at everything, so I decided to paint houses with my friend Billy. The first job was for a woman who owned a cottage elsewhere as a vacation home. One weekend when she was home, I went over and landed the job of staining her house. She wanted two colors of an exterior stain—one for the trim and one for the siding. We agreed on a price, and she asked me if I was clear on the colors or did I need a swatch of color applied to each area? Of course I was clear; I was fourteen! She had all the stain in the garage and went off to her cottage for the week, reminding me that she would be back the following weekend to check on the progress. Billy and I split the work. He started on the siding while I did the trim. It wasn't quite the end of the day when Billy came around to where I was working and announced that he was out of stain and there was no more in the garage. I thought that was strange because there should have been more of the siding color. So, being fourteen, I took charge, called the paint company to order more, and we kept on painting. I didn't notice that I had an enormous amount of my color left after the trim was done. And I didn't notice that the color scheme seemed odd. But when the owner came back the following weekend, she noticed. The colors were backwards! Fortunately she was a kind soul. We negotiated a way to fix the problem and reworked the job. My "expertise" and lack of a color sample nearly ruined us, and we were just starting our career! We lost our shirts! We also learned a lesson never forgotten, and I did get to that private school.

Using Japan Colors

These colors are extremely concentrated. When used full strength, they have a paint-like quality to them and dry matte. They are seldom used without diluting. They can be used at full strength to tint oil-based products such as the oil-based stains, colored oils, oil-based grain fillers, or oil-based gel stains. Or they can be diluted to make a stain, as described in the steps that follow. Japan colors are available in a dozen or more colors. By blending them, the combinations and color opportunities are endless!

Step 1: Open the can of Japan color and scoop out a tablespoon into a small cup.

Step 2: Add small amounts of solvent and stir. The most readily available appropriate solvent is mineral spirits. VM&P Naphtha is also appropriate if you want a quicker dry time. Try the mix on scraps, and continue to add solvent until the color density pleases you. Keep track of your formula for future mixes (see **Figure 4.20**).

Step 3: Apply the stain mixture with a rag or brush. Wipe off cleanly and streak free. Dispose of the rags immediately as described on page 14. If a deeper color is needed, wait 8 hours and stain again.

Step 4: Continue with the next step of finishing when thoroughly dry.

Tools and Materials
• Japan colors (pigment based)
• Mineral spirits or VM&P Naphtha

Figure 4.20. Add the solvent and stir. Be sure to keep track of the formula you used to achieve the desired mix.

Helpful Tip ─────────

Substituting Artist Oil Colors
Artist oil colors are similar to Japan colors but dry much more slowly. Anywhere a Japan color can be used an Artist oil can be substituted if you want, or don't mind, the longer dry time.

Don't Let Them Dry Up
These colors have strong driers in them and have a tendency to dry up in the container. Purchase small quantities and use them up quickly, before they dry up.

Using Base Tints

Base tints are universal colorants for tinting varnishes, lacquers, and epoxies. They are not appropriate for shellac or water-based products. You can make your own stains with them, as follows.

Tools and Materials

- Base tints (such as Behlen Master Colors or Croma-Chem 844 Colorants)
- Stain reducer (such as Behlen Wood Stain Reducer)

Step 1: Scoop about a tablespoon of base tint into a cup. Mix in stain reducer until the desired color density is achieved. You'll need to add four or more tablespoons of reducer to the tablespoon of base tint (see **Figure 4.21**).

Step 2: Apply as you would an oil-based stain, by rag or brush, and wipe off the excess cleanly. This stain mix dries very quickly; you can continue finishing within an hour.

Figure 4.21. Just like cooking in the kitchen, use a tablespoon and a cup to keep track of your portions for future mixing.

Primary colors: the fun stuff!

By now you've experienced the tendency of pigment stains to obscure the wood. Paint can be understood as a pigment stain with so much pigment in it that even a fairly thin coat will totally obscure the wood. If we thin down a paint so much that the pigment no longer totally obscures the wood, we will have a wood stain the color of the paint. How about a sky blue wood stain? How about a fire engine red stain on an oak picture frame for a clown picture in a kid's room? There's potential for some very exciting, very attractive, very happy results if done carefully in the right situation. And it can be a lot of fun!

In the exercises that follow, we'll be using water-based products (latex paint), oil-based products (Japan colors), and alcohol-based products (non-grain-raising stains), all in colors that you won't see growing on trees (unless, perhaps, it's a magnolia tree with purple blossoms) (see **Figure 4.22**).

Tools and Materials
- Panel or scrap of wood (hard or soft), 6" x 8"
- Mixing cups or jars
- Rags or brushes
- Measuring cups and spoons

Figure 4.22. With all these bright colors, you'll be having so much fun you will forget you are actually finishing!

Covered in this section:

Japan Color

page 80

Light Affects All Stains

page 81

Latex Paint

page 82

Compatible Color Products

page 83

Japan Color

Japan colors can provide the bright colors of latex paint but in an oil-based product. Woodburst Rainbow Colors are very similar to the Japan color recipe that follows, and the two can be mixed.

Tools and Materials
- Japan color, vermilion red
- Mineral spirits
- Tung oil or boiled linseed oil (optional)

Step 1: Scoop out a tablespoon or so of the pigment product into a container. Add enough mineral spirits to thin it to the desired color density. To make the stain more "slick," you can substitute pure tung oil or boiled linseed oil for some of the mineral spirits (see **Figure 4.23**).

Figure 4.23. The addition of oil to a mix of Japan color and spirits makes the mix spread more like an oil paint.

Non-Grain-Raising Primary Colors

Non-grain-raising stains in colors like bright red provide strong, vibrant colors that are completely transparent. The pigment-based colors are more paint-like. This is the big difference between dyes and pigments.

Use the primary color non-grain-raising stain (Solar-Lux or Mohawk) products as described in the section on using dye stains on page 70 (see **Figure 4.25**). I strongly recommend a retarder until you have considerable experience and can work fast. If the "canned" color of a non-grain-raising stain isn't quite right for your purposes, tweak it with concentrated dyes just as you would wood tones (see **Figure 4.26**).

Clearwater's water-based gel products are also available in primary colors and are much easier to use than the non-grain-raising stains. Application is somewhat "slippery," and this product doesn't evaporate as quickly. Still, it is good practice to work quickly to avoid any uneven color.

Once you have arrived at a group of colorants that you are comfortable working with, outfit your shop with the basic staining products and concentrated tinting products, such as the Japan colors or the two-ounce dye concentrates. There are 13 colors that you are most likely to find useful. The basic seven are black, white, red, blue, green, yellow, and orange. Supplement these with the wood tones—burnt umber, burnt sienna, raw umber, raw sienna, van dyke brown, and French ochre.

Figure 4.25. Primary color non-grain-raising stains are just an unconventional color of wood stain. Use them exactly as you would use the conventional colors.

Figure 4.26. You can tweak the primary color dye products with concentrated dyes just as you would tweak the conventional wood-tone dye products.

Step 2: Apply with a rag or brush. Wipe off cleanly (see **Figure 4.24**). Dry time can be as long as 10 to 12 hours if you added oil to the mix.

Figure 4.24. Application of your custom "stain" is the same as for proprietary oil stains: apply with a rag and wipe off the excess.

Light Affects All Stains

All stains fade when exposed to light, especially sunlight. The longer they are exposed, the more they fade. Dye stains fade more quickly than pigment stains, and water-soluble aniline dye stains fade more quickly than alcohol-soluble (non-grain-raising) aniline dye stains. **Figure 4.27** and **Figure 4.28** show the two types of aniline dye stains, water-soluble and alcohol-soluble (non-grain-raising), exposed to sun for six weeks. Pigment stains were not part of this exposure test.

UV protective additives in the topcoat can slow but not prevent fading. The finisher and the end-user need to understand the limitations and use finishing products and finished projects appropriately. For example, a dye should never be used on an exterior surface. A table in front of a south-facing window needs a tablecloth, or drapes on the window.

Figure 4.27. Both panels were stained with water-based aniline dyes. The left panel was shielded on the left side. The right panel was coated with three coats of exterior coating with UV filtering additives and the left side was shielded.

Figure 4.28. Both panels were stained with alcohol-based (non-grain-raising) aniline dye stains. The left panel was shielded on the left side. The right panel was coated with three coats of exterior coating with UV filtering additives and the left side was shielded.

CHAPTER 4 – COLORING WOOD

Say goodbye to wood stain color charts that fit on a 3 x 5 file card. Every neighborhood paint store has paint chip racks that would fill a truck. Every one of those colors can be diluted and used as a semi-transparent stain. Let the fun begin!

Tools and Materials

- Latex paint, bright red color (or ready-made stain such as General Finishes Country Colors, red)
- Water

Step 1: Scoop out a ½ cup of latex paint into a mixing cup or jar. Add enough water to begin the thinning process and mix thoroughly. Try the mix on a scrap. If a translucent effect is desired, the paint may have to be diluted 50%. If you want a wash effect, then dilute even more.

Step 2: Apply the diluted paint to the panel quickly by rag or brush. Wipe off cleanly (see **Figure 4.29**). Dry time is 8 hours.

Figure 4.29. Thinned latex paint can provide striking color while still showing wood grain.

Adventures in Finishing

Before we continue to the next section on glazes and color layering, I will tell you a story about an application for stain far beyond the realm of conventional woodworking.

A fellow from the Deep South called me one day and questioned me about the use of aniline dyes. He was curious to know if he could use these dyes on a couple of upholstered white couches on his front porch—spruce 'em up a little. I felt the sincerity of his question and replied respectfully by reminding him that anyone who sat on these couches with perspiration or white pants (or both) would have color all over them. In a backwoods drawl he agreed that it could be a problem. He came up with the brilliant solution of "urethaning" the couches wouldn't that work? I thought it might make crunchy noises, but asked him to let me know how the project turned out. I never did hear back from him . . .

Compatible Color Products

Pigments and tinting colors provide the wood finisher with great flexibility in producing perfect custom wood stains, but care must be taken to use tints and pigments that are compatible with the stains to be modified. With so many products on the market, keeping track of which ones are compatible can be confusing at best and a nightmare at worst. These photos group together the ones that work together.

Tint Minwax or Varathane oil-based stains with Japan colors, Artist oils, or Universal Tinting Colors.

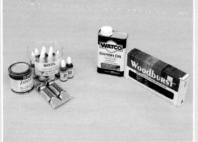

Tint Woodburst or Watco oils with Japan colors, Artist oils, or Universal Tinting Colors.

Tint water-based stains with Universal Tinting Colors or acrylic Artist colors.

Tint Behlen 15-Minute Stain with Master colors or Croma-Chem 844 Colorants.

Tint aniline dyes with other anilines of the same solvent category.

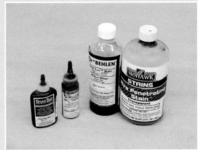

Tint Solar-Lux or Mohawk stains with TransTint or Wizard Tints.

Tint General gel stains or Bartley's gel with Japan colors, Artist oils, or other gel colors.

Tint Clearwater wood stains by mixing with other Clearwater wood stains.

Tint latex paints with Universal Tinting Colors or acrylic Artist colors.

Adding Glaze to a Three-Step Pine Test Sample

In the exercise on conditioning, page 44, we used a pine board and made a consistent, blotch-free color on it. However, the consequence of the conditioning created an overall lighter tone. Here, we are going to discover how, with the use of a glaze, to compensate for the lighter color.

Tools and Materials

- Shellac wash coat
- Behlen Shading and Glazing Stain, burnt umber, or General Finishes Water-based Glaze Effects, burnt umber
- 3-step pine test sample from the exercise on Conditioning with Shellac and Glue Size in Chapter 3: Preparing the Wood, page 44
- Aerosol sealer (optional)

Step 1: Apply a wash coat of shellac across all three sections. Allow them to dry 30 to 40 minutes, and then scuff gently with 320-grit abrasive on a block.

Step 2: Open the glaze and stir thoroughly. Brush a generous coat of the glaze across the surface (see **Figure 4.31**).

Step 3: It isn't necessary to wait; start wiping off the excess glaze in small circles, gently (see **Figure 4.32**). Turn the rag often to expose a clean, absorbent side. When most of the glaze is removed, finish off the panel with a rag, using long strokes in the direction of the grain. The goal is to leave a thin glaze of color on the surface. If the glaze is wiped off too vigorously, there will be no point to this exercise. Allow it to dry 4 to 6 hours.

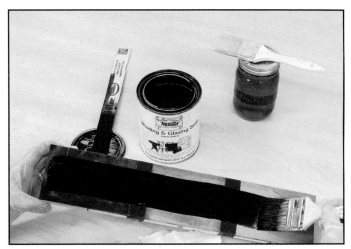

Figure 4.31. Brush the glaze on generously.

Figure 4.32. Gently wipe off the excess glaze.

Step 4: Once the glaze has dried, "lock down" the color with a wash coat. Again, be very careful applying the wash coat, working quickly and in one direction. If you are afraid of ruining all of that beautiful glazing, use an aerosol and lightly spray the surface to seal it. Now notice the subtle effect that the burnt umber has created on the pine (see **Figure 4.33**).

Step 5: When the wash coat is dry, scuff it gently with 320-grit abrasive. You can then apply a topcoat or add another layer of glaze. Multiple glaze layers can always be added as long as there is a wash coat between each one. Always wash coat the final glaze before topcoating.

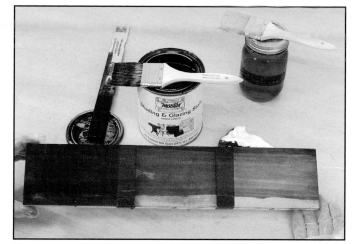

Figure 4.33. The effect is a subtle but definite improvement.

Helpful Tip _____

Gel Stain Alternative

A gel stain such as Bartley's can be substituted for the Behlen Shading and Glazing Stain. It should be applied over a scuffed wash coat. Work more quickly when removing the excess because the gel stain is sticky in comparison to the glazing stain.

A Recipe for Cherry

As promised, here is a recipe where we are thinking "out of the can"! We are going to start with no base color on a panel.

Tools and Materials
- Cherry panel
- Shellac wash coat
- Burnt umber glazing stain

Step 1: Apply a wash coat of shellac to a sanded and tacked off cherry panel (see **Figure 4.34**). Allow it to dry and scuff it gently with 320-grit abrasive.

Step 2: Apply the glaze to the panel, and then remove the excess by wiping it off gently with a rag in small circles. Turn the rag often to a clean, absorbent side. Finish off the panel with a rag, using long strokes in the direction of the grain, leaving a thin layer of color on the surface. Notice the beautiful, even color of the cherry (see **Figure 4.35**). The tone of the cherry can be altered by choosing a different glaze color. For instance, dark mahogany glaze will provide a more "rosy" tone to the cherry.

Step 3: Lock down the glaze layer with a carefully applied wash coat before continuing with a topcoat.

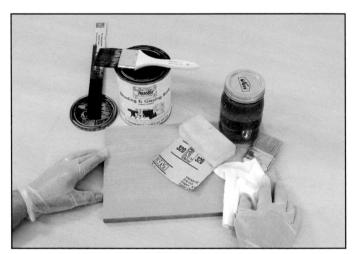

Figure 4.34. Start with a wash coat but no color.

Figure 4.35. Notice how even the color is!

The Difference a Glaze Makes

In Chapter 3: Preparing the Wood, in the section on Filling the Grain, page 50, we went through Making a Four-Part Test Board with Conventional Grain Filler to produce a four-section test sample showing the effects of stains, grain fillers, and wash coats on an oak panel. The last step ended with the line, "Let it dry before continuing with more color or topcoating." If you wondered at the time, "What more could be done with color?" the answer is here—your four-step test sample now with the upper half treated to a burnt umber glaze (see **Figure 4.36**).

Note that these eight distinct effects are all on the same piece of oak plywood, and we've used only two colors, a golden oak stain and burnt umber grain filler and glaze. The possibilities really are endless.

Figure 4.36. Note how the glaze created a more even tone on top.

The bottom four sections of the panel have received, from left to right, the following sequence of finishes:			
– –	– –	NGR golden oak stain	NGR golden oak stain
– –	Wash coat	– –	Wash coat
Burnt umber grain filler	Burnt umber grain filler	Burnt umber grain filler	Burnt umber grain filler
Wash coat	Wash coat	Wash coat	Wash coat

In addition to the above finishes, the top four sections have all received a burnt umber glaze.

Adventures in Finishing

Continue on into the next finish adventure with topcoats, but first let me tell you about my discovery of glazes (and I didn't even know it!).

I was in my twenties and first married, when we had plenty of time but no money. In New England, the antiques business was booming. Dealers from California and southern states like Georgia and the Carolinas were buying up and trucking off all the antiques they could find. Estate sales in those days weren't attended by many retail folks, so poor dealers like us could fill a pickup truck for a hundred dollars. We would buy up all the broken stuff over the weekend, and on Monday morning we'd make up a listing of twenty or more pieces for our auctioneer for the following Friday night sale. It took imagination. We might be looking at a broken-down old dry sink, missing a door, with rat holes chewed in the bottom, and write in our listing, "Beautiful country dry sink in pine, rare original form, perfect condition." Then by working like crazy for four days, the twenty items were repaired and finished, transformed into great antiques.

The challenge was getting it all done on time. It might be Thursday night or Friday morning before we completed the repairs, and we still had to blend them in and apply finishes. And the auction was that night! Never daunted, I would apply some shellac and stain and some more shellac, letting things dry just barely enough! Then to get everything looking just right, I would scoop the muck from the bottom of my Minwax stain cans and smear it over the section to be blended. (I didn't know at the time that I was actually glazing!) After wiping off carefully and spraying a bit of urethane over it, I would dust it with a little rottenstone to age it, and the piece was done! Final drying was open-air on the back of the pickup on the way to the sale!

CHAPTER 5

TOPCOATING

Topcoats provide a protective shield on wood that keeps dirt, grime, water, and scuffing damage to a minimum. There are many kinds of topcoats to choose from, providing varying degrees of protection to meet varying needs and suited for several methods of application. There is a topcoat to meet the preferences of just about any woodworker.

Choosing among topcoats is seldom simple. Each has unique characteristics, some of which can be considered advantages or disadvantages, but others are just differences that may be preferable in some situations but not in others. For example, solvents so strong that you have to use a respirator to apply the finish would be considered a disadvantage to be endured only in order to gain some other advantage. But a finish that "warms" the color of the wood may be desirable in some cases and undesirable in others. Just to round out the complexity, you, the finisher, are one of the variables. For example, some of you have, or will discover, a strong preference for brushing while others will always prefer wiping on a finish.

The exercises that follow will equip you to make good decisions by providing experience in all of the basic types of topcoats and two of the three application methods, brushing and wiping. Spraying is for another book. I urge you to do all of the exercises. You may discover a liking for a topcoat that you've never considered, and, even if you don't, you'll have experience backing up your decision not to use it again.

I've grouped the exercises first by application method, then by composition of the finish within the application method. You'll find explanations of the advantages, disadvantages, and differences of each as you go along.

Brush-on topcoats

Compared to wipe-on products, topcoat products intended for brushing have less solvent in them and are therefore thicker, more syrupy, and less watery. This "heaviness" has two consequences; the layer of product that you apply is thicker, and the part of the product that remains as a dry film is greater. Both of these outcomes result in a thicker layer of protection with each coat. You get more protection with less time and effort. (see **Figure 5.1**)

Figure 5.1. These photos show the tools and materials essential for brushing out water-based (left) and oil-based (right) topcoats.

Tools and Materials

- Portable shop light or very good overhead lighting
- 1-quart mixing containers
- Stir sticks
- Disposable cups (recyclable plastic cups)
- Fine paint filters
- Panel or scrap of wood (hard or soft), 6" x 8"
- Felt and cork or wood sanding blocks
- 220- and 320-grit abrasive paper (sheets or 3M Stikit self-adhesive abrasive paper)
- Tack cloth
- Rags, preferably washed cotton T-shirt material
- Masters Brush Cleaner
- Spritzer bottle with water

Covered in this section:

Brushing Oil-Based Urethane
page 94

Brushing Water-Based Urethane
page 96

Brushing On Shellac
page 98

Brushing On Lacquer
page 100

Brushing Oil-Based Urethane

Oil-based coatings warm the color of the wood and are very durable, but brushing them on is a challenge. The manufacturers of the products present the process as easy—anyone can have a gorgeous finish with hardly any effort. In reality, it is nearly impossible to get a flawless finish right off the brush. There! I said it! The big difficulty is that oil-based products are so slow drying that every bit of dust in the air has time to settle into the wet film. To fix it, you then have to "rub out" the finish as described on page 120. Rubbing out amounts to "finishing" the finish and truly results in a gorgeous finish, but takes a lot of time and effort.

Step 1: Clean the finishing area thoroughly, including spraying the floor with water to minimize dust (see **Figure 5.2**). Make sure the room temperature is comfortable for you. If it's comfortable for you, the finish will work the way it's supposed to. Cover your work surface with paper or plastic, and support your practice panel up off the bench with scraps of wood, as shown in **Figure 5.3**. Make sure the panel has been tacked off.

Step 2: Open the can of finish and stir it gently. The directions will tell you if it needs thinning. (The first coat is usually thinned to become a sealer.) Pour enough of the finish to cover the panel through a paint filter into a cup.

Step 3: Condition the brush by dipping it into mineral spirits right up to the hilt (ferrule). I prefer mixing containers from the paint store for this operation (see **Figure 5.4**). Squeeze excess mineral spirits out of the brush into a rag.

Step 4: Dip the brush approximately one-third into the finish. Press the brush against the side of the cup to drain off the excess.

Step 5: Do not start at the very end of the panel! It will scrape the finish off the brush and drool down the side, especially if it isn't a practice panel! Instead, start about a third to a quarter of the way in from the end and brush in one direction. Then immediately brush back toward the opposite end (see **Figure 5.5**). Continue in this fashion over the whole panel.

Tools and Materials

- 2"-wide badger or lorient brush (see Brushes and their Care sidebar on page 10)
- Urethane topcoat (such as Waterlox XL 88, 89, or Minwax polyurethane in your choice of satin or gloss)
- Mineral spirits
- Lacquer thinner
- Paper or plastic to cover work area
- Scraps of wood

Figure 5.2. Spritz the floor with water to settle the dust.

Figure 5.3. Support your work piece above your bench when brushing topcoats. Tack off just before finishing.

Step 6: Remove as much of the finish as you can from the brush by raking it across the edge of the cup. Now tip off the surface by angling the brush at 45 degrees to the surface and gently stroking out any puddles or dry areas. The purpose of tipping off is to gently reflow the material that you just applied to a more even, stroke-free, and puddle-free surface. Tipping off will also soak up some excess material.

Step 7: Walk away! Even after the panel has been tipped off and looks reasonably good, it is tempting to fool with it more. Don't. Let it settle and dry, at least 8 hours for most oil-based products.

Step 8: Now clean the brush as described for oil-based products in Brushes and their Care on page 10.

Step 9: When the first coat is dry, apply a second and a third coat. Additional coats start with a scuff of 220- or 320-grit abrasive on a felt block. (The 220 might be necessary if there is a lot of debris in the surface). Tack off and apply the additional coats in exactly the same manner as the first coat. *Condition and clean the brush each and every time!*

Step 10: Before the last of at least three to four coats, the panel needs a thorough scuffing that is best described as "leveling"—sanding out brush marks, dust nubbins, and any other problems. The leveling can be done with wet/dry abrasive paper wrapped around a cork or wood block and a lubricant such as mineral spirits. Stop frequently and wipe the panel clean to check on your progress. The goal is a surface that has very few shiny (low) spots, but you don't want to remove more finish than you have to.

Step 11: Apply the final coat as you did the previous coats, being as careful as possible. If you have chosen a gloss sheen, the next step will be a full rub-out; if a satin sheen was chosen, a soft or "simple" rub-out is all that is needed. Rubbing out is described on page 122.

Figure 5.4. Condition your brush with a soak in mineral spirits, and then set the spirits aside for cleaning the brush when you're done.

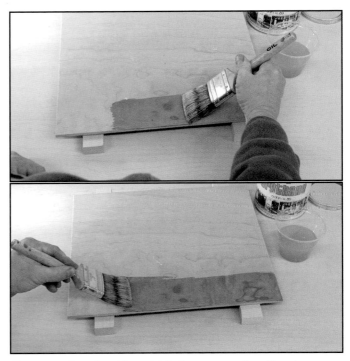

Figure 5.5. Start brushing a bit in from one end and brush to the opposite end; then reverse and brush all the way back to the first end.

Helpful Tip

Angling the Light
Position the light so it shines down and toward you from the far side of your work surface, reflecting off of the wet coating.

Brushing Water-Based Urethane

Brushing water-based urethane is attractive because the odor is minimal, both the product and the cleanup are less toxic than oil-based urethane, and it dries faster than its oil-based counterpart. These are big advantages.

The other side of the coin includes the "cold" or "plastic-looking" appearance of water-based coatings and the tendency of any finish with water in it to raise the grain. The grain raising issue will be dealt with in this exercise.

The appearance issue is subjective and depends in part on the wood itself. We're accustomed to traditional oil-based finishes that "warm up" the wood, giving much the same appearance as exposure of the wood to light over time.

While water-based urethanes do not warm up the wood like oil does, in some projects that could be desirable. For instance, maple is a beautiful creamy white when first exposed. To keep that appearance, the water-based product is perfect. The best way to decide for yourself is to accumulate ten years of experience with both types of finish. If you don't have ten years, make test samples with both oil- and water-based topcoats and prop them against a south-facing window for as long as you have.

Tools and Materials
- 2"-wide Taklon or Moser's Choice brush
- Shellac wash coat
- Concentrated dye tint (such as Trans Tint or Wizard Tints)
- Water-based urethane (such as General Polyacrylic Blend or Moser's Simple Success)
- Household ammonia (not lemon scented)
- Tack cloth specifically for water-based finishes (or a damp cloth)

Step 1: Clean the finishing area as described for applying oil-based urethanes, on page 94. Set up the panel on strips of wood and tack off with a tack cloth specifically designed for water-based products or a slightly damp rag.

Step 2: Apply an even wash coat of shellac (see **Figure 5.6**). If the wood needs "warming up," put a drop or two of concentrated dye tint into the wash coat (see **Figure 5.7**). Depending on the wood, choose a honey amber, walnut, or reddish tone such as bordeaux. Test the mix on a scrap to be sure. Let the wash coat dry and scuff gently with 320-grit abrasive on a block.

Step 3: Open the can of water-based urethane and stir gently. If a satin or semigloss sheen has been chosen, there will be sludge in the bottom of the can. This is the flattening agent that determines the sheen. Make sure it is completely blended in. Pour the stirred material into a cup through a paint filter.

Step 4: Condition the brush by submerging it into water (see **Figure 5.8**). Squeeze out the excess water gently with a rag.

Figure 5.6. Begin with a wash coat to prevent the grain from raising when the water-based urethane goes onto the wood.

Helpful Tip _____

Oils and Water-Based Topcoats
Oils can sometimes play havoc with water-based topcoats. A shellac wash coat over an oil product will prevent trouble.

Step 5: Dip the brush approximately one-third of the way into the urethane. Gently press the brush against the cup to avoid bubbles and foam. Start a third of the way into the panel and brush to the far end. The Taklon brush does not hold a lot of the urethane, so, if need be, reload the brush before coming back in the opposite direction to finish the strip (see **Figure 5.9**). Continue down the panel. Tip off once and leave it alone!

Step 6: Now clean the brush as described for water-based products in Brushes and their Care on page 10.

Step 7: To recoat, lightly scuff the panel with 320-grit abrasive on a felt block, tack off, and repeat Steps 3 through 7. Three to four coats is usually sufficient.

Helpful Tip

Using Foam Brushes

Foam brushes are very popular, and some folks have the impression that they are easy to use and are foolproof. They will do, but they are not perfect. If you decide not to invest in the more expensive brushes in these exercises, be aware that foam brushes have a dark side to them. They soak up a lot of material, but then there is no control over the amount of material being laid down. And during the trip from the can, the brush can suddenly leak an amazing amount of material across your bench and panel, as shown in **Figure 5.10**.

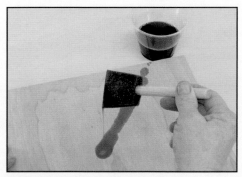

Figure 5.10. The downside to foam brushes is an irritating tendency to drip.

Figure 5.7. Since the water-based urethane won't warm the wood, a drop or two of dye tint in a wash coat may be desirable.

Figure 5.8. Submerge the brush in water to condition it.

Figure 5.9. Never start brushing at an end; always brush toward an end.

Brushing On Shellac

Shellac is an ancient, natural material that has been used for centuries. These days it provides benefits in unlikely products including no-wax floor finishes, cosmetics, food (as a confectionary coating), pills, and hair spray (see **Figure 5.11**). Shellac as a wood finish holds a prestigious position as the material in French polishing. As a brush-on finish, it can produce a beautiful, soft shine. It is easy to work with, is non-toxic when dry, dries quickly, warms up the color of the wood, and is unique as a conditioner and as a barrier coat between layers of color.

Shellac's weak point is poor durability. It has no resistance to alcohol and very low resistance to water and scuffing. The bright side of any damage is ease of repair.

This exercise will show how to apply shellac by brush. We will be using Bullseye Sealcoat, which is a product ready for use right out of the can. If you want to mix your own shellac flakes, see the Mixing your Own Shellac from Flakes section on page 148.

Tools and Materials

- 2" Taklon or Moser's Choice brush dedicated to shellac
- Prepared, 2-pound cut, dewaxed shellac (such as Bullseye Sealcoat)
- Mineral oil
- Mineral spirits
- Denatured alcohol
- Household ammonia
- 320- and 400-grit wet/dry abrasive paper

Step 1: As in the previous steps, start with a clean finishing area, good lighting, and a practice panel on support blocks. Tack off the surface.

Step 2: Open the can of shellac and stir well. The material in the can is a 2-pound cut, which is a good consistency for brushing. However, if you are new to brushing out shellac, you may want to thin it with denatured alcohol. For roughly a 1-pound cut, mix one part Sealcoat to one part alcohol (see **Figure 5.12**). Thinning does not affect the shellac; the coats are just thinner, so it takes more of them to build up.

Step 3: The Taklon brush you use for shellac should be permanently dedicated to shellac. There is no need to condition it as in the previous exercises. Simply dip the brush into the shellac and begin the same brushing technique as in the previous exercises— start a third of the way into the panel, brush to the other end and then back (see **Figure 5.13**). Work quickly and reload often. This brush does not hold a huge reservoir of material, but the super-fine bristles lay down shellac superbly.

Figure 5.11. Shellac is versatile, used in products as varied as food, medications, cosmetics, and floor maintenance products.

Figure 5.12. When first getting started with shellac, thin it 1:1 just as you would for a wash coat.

Step 4: The first coat goes on easily and soaks in rapidly. It will need a gentle scuffing with 320-grit abrasive and tacking off before the second coat. Be aware that the second coat is not going to glide across the surface as easily as the first. A new coat of shellac softens the previous coat, so every brush full of shellac must be laid down quickly, with little rebrushing. Dry time is determined by how tacky it feels. As soon as it can be scuffed without the sandpaper catching or dragging, another coat can be applied.

Step 5: As the coats build (five to ten is not unusual), the appearance of your panel goes downhill. There will be areas heavier than others, maybe puddles, and ridges (see **Figure 5.14**). These problems can be solved as you approach the final two to three coats. Let the panel rest for 8 hours. Begin leveling by wet sanding with 320- or 400-grit wet/dry paper on a cork block and a lubricant made from one part mineral oil and one part mineral spirits. Spritz the lubricant onto the panel and begin sanding. Wipe off the slurry frequently to check the progress. The goal is to have few, if any, shiny spots.

Step 6: Thoroughly wipe off any residue of the lubricant with a clean rag. Set up and apply the final two to three coats; then leave the panel alone until it's fully hardened and doesn't feel tacky or gummy. The build of shellac is now ready for rub-out. See page 120 for the complete step-by-step rub-out process.

Step 7: Cleaning the brush isn't necessary, as mentioned in Brushes and their Care on page 10. Just lay it flat on a clean surface. The brush will tend to harden between coats but will soften up nicely after sitting in a cup of shellac for 10 or 15 minutes (see **Figure 5.15**).

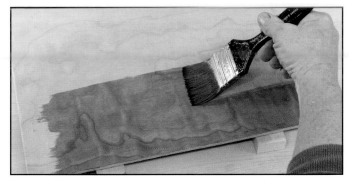

Figure 5.13. Brushing shellac with a super-fine bristle brush is a real pleasure. Remember to start a third of the way into the panel.

Figure 5.14. A neglected puddle, to be dealt with when "leveling."

Figure 5.15. Another reason finishers love shellac: Instead of cleaning the brush every time you use it, just let it harden and then soak it in shellac for fifteen minutes the next time you need it.

Helpful Tip

How Many Coats of Shellac?

Some finishers keep the number of shellac coats low—three to four at most. They then scuff and rub out with fine steel wool and paste wax. This is a great way to finish small projects that don't need a full film finish for protection or a high sheen (**see Figure 5.16**).

Figure 5.16. Shellac and then wax make a great combination for small projects that won't receive a lot of abuse.

Brushing On Lacquer

Brushing lacquer provides better protection than shellac, but it's more difficult to apply. Each brush full almost immediately dissolves the previous coat on contact. Knowing that, it's important to work quickly without overbrushing or tipping off. Just flow the material on. All the problems will be "fixed" during leveling and rubbing out.

Tools and Materials
- 2" badger or lorient brush dedicated to lacquer
- Respirator
- Brushing lacquer (such as Deft or Behlen)
- Brushing lacquer thinner

Step 1: Set up the work space and practice panel as in the previous exercises with one addition: provide very good ventilation. Brushing lacquer has strong solvents in it that will cause lightheadedness. Wear a respirator if you have any doubt at all.

Step 2: Thin the lacquer about 10% with the thinner recommended by the manufacturer. This will allow the lacquer to flow better (see **Figure 5.17**).

Step 3: Condition the badger or lorient brush by submerging it in lacquer thinner. Squeeze out the excess in a clean rag.

Figure 5.17. Thin the lacquer to your preferred brushing consistency; 10% is a good starting point if this is your first experience with it.

Step 4: Load the brush with lacquer and begin brushing. Start several inches from an end and continue to the opposite end. Come right back and finish to the end in the other direction. Work fast, keep the brush well loaded, and maintain a wet edge. Quickly stroke through any puddles and keep going. When you're done, park your brush in lacquer thinner, and allow an hour for the lacquer to dry to the touch before continuing (see **Figure 5.18**). (Clean the brush as described in Brushes and their Care on page 10 if you'll be gone longer.)

Step 5: Apply at least four coats and level the panel just before the final coat. Use the same leveling procedures and materials as in Steps 5 and 6 in Brushing On Shellac on page 99. Apply the final coat as pristinely as possible.

Step 6: Now clean the brush as described for lacquer in Brushes and their Care on page 10.

Step 7: When the buildup of lacquer is thoroughly hard (three or more days), rub it out as described on page 120.

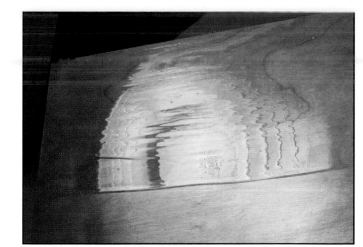

Figure 5.18. Don't expect perfection when lacquer is first brushed on; it dries too fast. You'll deal with brush strokes and other irregularities after it dries.

Adventures in Finishing

This concludes the section on brushing on topcoats. The next section is devoted to wiping on finishes, but first let me tell you about a skeptical student.

The class was on my favorite subject: shellac. We were going over the various problems with brushing out a shellac finish. When I mentioned that shellac was a dream to spray compared to brushing, one of my purist students challenged me. He said that he had been brushing it for years and, though admittedly slow, it was just fine. His clients appreciated the tradition of a hand-rubbed shellac finish. The gauntlet had been thrown down, and I picked it up. With spray gun in hand, I asked him if he wanted me to demonstrate how efficient it was by spraying shellac on a practice panel. Smugly he agreed. Into the spray booth we went and in 30 minutes I had six light coats built up, and they looked almost 100% defect free. There was silence as the awe ran across his face. Brushing on six coats would have taken hours, and they definitely would have had flaws. The big light bulb went on, and I knew someone was going to go shopping for a spray gun! All those years of brushing . . .

Wipe-on topcoats

Of all the film finishes, the wipe-on products are the most popular. They are fairly foolproof and simple to use, but they take time to build a decent layer simply because each application adds a minimal amount of material to the surface. A brushed-on finish is adequate after two or three coats, but a wipe-on needs at least double that for a durable surface.

This section will cover several oil-based products as well as one non-oil: shellac (see **Figure 5.19**). When working with oil-based wipe-on finishes, always take care of the oily rags immediately! Left in a heap on your bench, these rags can burst into flames in less than 15 minutes. Be careful (see the Safety section on page 12)!

Tools and Materials

- Good backlighting
- Good ventilation
- Disposable gloves
- Panel or scrap of wood (hard or soft), 6" x 8"
- Cups or jars
- Rags (clean old T-shirts are best)
- Felt sanding block
- Fine abrasives, 320- or 400-grit
- Tack cloth

Figure 5.19. Wipe-on topcoats require few tools, but the oil-based ones require a safe means of disposing of oily rags such as the approved oily waste can, shown. Good backlighting, good ventilation, and disposable gloves are important regardless of the specific product type.

Covered in this Section:

Wiping On Varnish

Wipe-on varnishes provide more of a surface film than wipe-on oils, which tend to penetrate more, but don't build up as quickly as brush-on finishes. Think of them as a middle ground.

Tools and Materials

• Wipe-on varnish (such as Waterlox Original Sealer, Watco Wipe-On Poly, or General Finishes Seal-A-Cell, clear)

Step 1: Pour an adequate amount of your chosen wipe-on varnish into a cup or jar.

Step 2: Flood the panel with a moderate amount of the product and spread it around with a rag (see **Figure 5.20**).

Step 3: Let the material soak in and reapply wherever there are dry spots. After 15 to 30 minutes, wipe off the excess and take care of your rags! While drying time is not critical, wait 4 to 8 hours or more before continuing.

Step 4: Scuff gently with 320- or 400-grit abrasive. Tack off the dust and reapply as in Steps 2 and 3 for as many applications as you like. More coats provide more protection. When fully dry and cured for a week or more, follow the instructions for a soft rub-out on page 122.

Figure 5.20. Applying a wipe-on finish is not high-tech. Just flood the surface and then spread it around.

Helpful Tip

Prevent Wiping Varnishes from Drying Up

Wiping varnishes have a nasty habit of gelling up in the can. No amount of thinner will reconstitute these products because they have started to cure in the can. A product called Bloxygen is designed to prevent this from happening. Each and every time the can is opened, squirt a four-second blast of Bloxygen into it, as shown in **Figure 5.21**, and close the cover quickly. The heavier-than-air gases prevent oxygen from reacting with the product, and I promise that you will reach the end of the can before throwing it out.

Figure 5.21. Bloxygen prevents partial curing of finishes in the can between uses. It really does work.

Applying Danish Oil Conventionally

Danish oils (sometimes called penetrating oils) warm, or mellow, the color of the wood but do not obscure the texture of the wood as much as finishes that create more of a film. While this may sound appealing (and is, to many), they provide only minimal protection to the wood, quickly acquiring a "comfortable old jeans" look if they are handled regularly.

Tools and Materials

- Danish oil (such as Deft, Olympic, Watco, and others)

Step 1: Pour a puddle or pool of the oil onto the panel. Wipe it around with a rag until the entire surface is wet (see **Figure 5.22**). Allow it to sit and penetrate for 30 minutes or so and wipe off the excess.

Step 2: Take care of your rags immediately. Repeat the application after letting the oil dry for 8 hours or so. This is the basic application method for applying all Danish oils until several coats have built up on the surface.

Figure 5.22. Pour it on and spread it around; oils apply easily.

Adventures in Finishing

Keep right on oiling, but, while it's drying, let me tell you a story about a wipe-on finish that wasn't easy for one gentleman.

This fine citizen called me and was very upset. Someone had told him that gel varnish was simple to use, so he used it on a table. After four days it still wasn't dry! By talking with him, I eliminated humidity and temperature as possible problems. Then I asked him how it was applied. He retorted, "With a brush, of course!" I asked him what he did next, and he said, "Whadaya mean, what did I do next? Nothing! It isn't dry!"

At this point, I directed him to the side of the can, which advised the user to apply and then wipe off all of the excess. I think he took a trip to the store for a wide-blade putty knife to push off all that gel . . .

I can only imagine a tabletop with all of that jellylike finish on it, just sitting there not drying. In this case the simplest part of the product was reading the directions first!

Wet Sanding Danish Oil

Only slightly more involved than the simple instructions on the can, wet sanding Danish oil produces a smoother surface. The popularity of Danish oil as a finish is often attributed to its "minimalist" appearance and sometimes to its ease of application. But another appeal may be its flexibility, as demonstrated by this exercise in wet sanding with it. I've also heard of woodworkers who use ultra-fine Scotchbrite pads to rub it in.

Tools and Materials
- Felt block with 400-grit wet/dry sandpaper
- Danish oil (such as Deft, Olympic, Watco, and others)

Step 1: Pour out a puddle of material onto the panel. Wrap a felt block with 400-grit wet/dry sandpaper and begin sanding the oil into the wood (see **Figure 5.23**). As the oil is driven into the wood, the friction increases.

Step 2: When the oil is almost gone, wipe off the leftover slurry and reapply another puddle. Wet sand that in as well.

Step 3: Wipe the almost-dry slurry off and let the panel rest for 8 or more hours. Notice how incredibly smooth the surface is using this technique.

Step 4: For the next two to four coats, simply apply the Danish oil as in Apply Danish Oil Conventionally on page 105.

Step 5: When the coats of oil have finally cured, a simple rub-out with fine steel wool and wax (see page 122) will create a silky, soft surface.

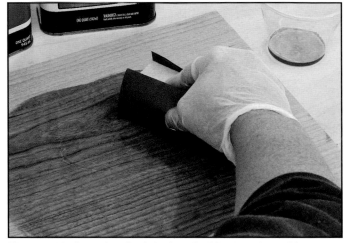

Figure 5.23. Spread and rub in the oil with 400-grit wet/dry sandpaper for an exceptionally smooth final result.

Helpful Tip

Preventing Oils from Popping Back Out of the Grain
On open-grained woods such as oak or ash, penetrating oils have a nasty habit of "popping" back out of the grain. It will happen after the oil has begun to dry (and you have gone in for the night). Little spots of oil that were deep in the pores of the wide-open grain want to come out and, if left too long, actually dry hard. The best way to avoid this problem is to either avoid flooding on the first two coats and simply wipe thin coats on or apply a very thin wash coat of shellac first. If spots of oil have already hardened, as shown in **Figure 5.24**, wet sand them with 400-grit abrasive and the same oil you were finishing with to remove them.

Figure 5.24. Oil that "pops" out of the grain and is allowed to dry, as shown here, can be removed by wet sanding.

Applying Gel Varnish

Gel varnish is very similar to wipe-on varnish in the final result. The only significant difference is that it penetrates less. That can be an important difference on woods with variable absorbency. If you've done a test sample with wipe-on varnish and have been disappointed with inconsistent results, try gel varnish. The other big difference is in application. Applying the gel is like spreading mayonnaise while applying wipe-on is more like spreading maple syrup.

Tools and Materials

- Gel varnish (such as Bartley's clear satin, Behlen's Master Gel)
- Paint stick

Step 1: Open the can of gel varnish, but don't stir it. It has a jellylike consistency that will liquefy if stirred; then, you'll have to let it sit to re-gel. With a brush or paint stick, scoop out enough gel varnish to cover the surface (see **Figure 5.25**).

Step 2: Spread the material over the panel with a rag or chip brush. Work quickly because the gel becomes sticky. Remove all excess with a rag. When you are done, a thin skim of gel should be all that is on the panel. Allow it to dry; most gel varnishes require 8 hours or more.

Step 3: Scuff gently with 320-grit abrasive on a felt block. Tack off and apply a second coat in exactly the same manner as the first coat. At least four coats should be applied to build durability.

Step 4: The sheen of gel varnishes is usually satin. To finish the finish, wait three to four days, and then follow the soft rub-out outlined on page 122.

Figure 5.25. Scoop the product onto the workpiece; as a gel, it won't pour conveniently.

Helpful Tip

Getting Durability with Gel Varnishes

The gel varnishes are wonderful to work with but have the same drawback as other wipe-on finishes; their durability has been compromised both by thinning it enough to be a wipe-on and by actually applying such a small amount with each coat. For a tabletop, either double the number of gel varnish coats or use a traditional brush-on urethane.

Applying Shellac as a Wipe-On

Carved work or complicated moldings can be difficult to finish with a brush without a lot of drips and runs or excessive finish in deep recesses. In such cases, wiping on a finish may allow more control. This exercise will equip you with some experience in wiping on shellac before you tackle a project with complicated shapes.

Tools and Materials
- 2-pound cut, dewaxed shellac (such as Bullseye Sealcoat)
- Denatured alcohol

Step 1: The shellac must be reduced with denatured alcohol to allow an easy wipe-on application. The best mix is a one to one ratio of 2-pound cut shellac and alcohol, the same dilution we've been using as a wash coat.

Step 2: Dip into a cup of diluted shellac with a clean rag, and let it soak up enough to be thoroughly wet but not dripping. Wipe it on rapidly in the direction of the grain. Do not overwipe because it will pull up any that has already started to dry (see **Figure 5.26**). Continue this process two or three times over the panel, and then let it rest.

Step 3: Scuff very gently with 400-grit abrasive on a felt block; then, continue with more applications.

Figure 5.26. When wiping on shellac, work quickly before it dries.

Helpful Tip _____

Wipe-On Shellac as a Final Finish
This process is ideal for putting down a controlled wash coat or for thinly applying shellac to intricate or vertical spindles. It is not easy to build a final finish with this method. The following process, padding on shellac, is more suitable for that.

Padding On Shellac

The technique described here is a somewhat more controlled version of wiping on shellac. Padding on shellac is ideal for flat surfaces. For other parts of a piece of furniture, the shellac must be thinly brushed out in multiple coats (see page 98 for brushing on shellac.) When the entire project has enough "build" of shellac, it can be rubbed out with fine steel wool and wax.

That will do it for wiping on the most popular finishes. Refer to the Recipes section on page 132 for the secret three-part formulas that no one wants to tell you about.

Tools and Materials

- 2-pound cut, dewaxed shellac (such as Bullseye Sealcoat)
- Denatured alcohol
- Double-sided tape or nails
- Brown paper
- 600-grit abrasive paper
- Measuring spoons

Step 1: Secure the practice panel firmly to the bench. If it is just scrap, use double-stick tape or nail it down. If it is a part from a project, attach cleats to the bottom and clamp those to the bench.

Step 2: Make the applicator "tool" with a wad of old washed T-shirt material wrapped snugly in an outer layer of the same material (see **Figure 5.27**). The bottom of the pad should be wrinkle free.

Figure 5.27. The "pad" for padding shellac consists of a wad of T-shirt material wrapped in the same material.

Step 3: Squirt a tablespoon of alcohol and twice that of the shellac into the pad. On a piece of brown paper, tamp the pad a few times to moisturize the whole pad (see **Figure 5.28**).

Step 4: Wipe a generous amount over the surface, even it out, and let it dry. Scuff it with 400-grit abrasive on a block and tack it off.

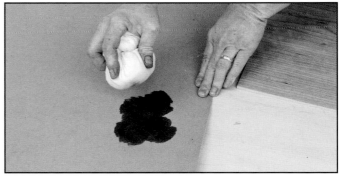

Figure 5.28. Tamping the pad distributes the finish throughout the pad.

Step 5: Reload the pad in the same way, and tamp off any dripping excess on the brown paper. Begin padding by coming into the panel and skidding across the entire piece to the opposite side and lifting off. Come back across the same section rapidly and progress down the panel, reloading as soon as the pad feels sticky (see **Figure 5.29**).

Step 6: This process can be repeated until a satisfactory finish is achieved. If at any time streaks or problems arise, stop, let the panel harden, and gently level with 400- or 600-grit abrasive paper.

Figure 5.29. Each "sweep" with the wet pad adds another thin layer to the finish.

Painting wood

Painting a piece of furniture seems like heresy to some woodworkers. However, there are occasions when the wood is inferior, the client desires a certain look, or the style demands a painted surface. Some also think that paint is "easy" or somehow "less than" a natural wood finish, but nothing could be further from the truth! A quality painted surface is much more difficult to achieve than a clear finish.

Professional finishers with spray equipment have an advantage when it comes to applying a colored finish. They don't have to use paint. Instead they use a pigmented lacquer that can be sprayed "like mist on the moor" to achieve a gorgeous, flawless, "painted" surface. A Steinway piano with a black finish is a perfect example of the highest-quality colored finish (see **Figure 5.30**).

Figure 5.30. Paint can provide a very high-quality finish, as evidenced by this piano's black finish.

Covered in this section:

Modern Latex Paint as a Fine Finish
page 112

Milk Paint Sample Board
page 114

Distressed Two-Color Milk Paint Panel
page 116

More on Painting
page 119

Modern Latex Paint as a Fine Finish

Usually, a paint job looks like brushed-out paint. This exercise shows a great way to acquire a furniture-grade finish with paint.

Tools and Materials
- Palette/putty knife
- Best available flagged tip synthetic bristle 2" latex paintbrush
- 220- and 320-grit abrasive paper
- Sanding block
- Test sample board of pine or poplar, 4" x 16" or so, sanded up to 220
- Wood putty and/or Bondo
- Vinyl spackle
- Pigmented shellac primer (such as Bin)
- Best latex paint available (in any color)
- Water-based clear finish (such as Simple Success or Minwax)
- Household ammonia
- Brush cleaner
- Tack cloth
- Water

Step 1: Fill all voids, knotholes, and defects with wood putty as described in Chapter 3 on page 30. Or, if they are too large for wood putty, use Bondo (see **Figure 5.31**).

Step 2: Allow the filler to dry hard. Sand the board up to 220 grit as described in Chapter 3 on page 28. Vacuum up all of the dust, and check the surface for flaws with backlighting and solvent.

Step 3: Open and thoroughly stir the pigmented shellac primer. Brush an even coat onto the board as described for Brushing On Shellac on page 98 (see **Figure 5.32**).

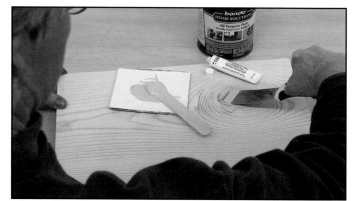

Figure 5.31. Quality painted finishes begin with a perfectly smooth surface. Fill all imperfections.

Figure 5.32. Seal and prime the sanded, fault-free surface with a shellac-based primer.

Step 4: Allow the primer to dry and sand it smooth with 320-grit abrasive paper on a block. Apply a second coat of primer, let it dry, and sand again.

Step 5: Inspect the surface thoroughly for imperfections. If there are any voids still left, fill them in with spackle. When the spackle is dry, final sand with a block and 320-grit abrasive (see **Figure 5.33**).

Step 6: Tack off the surface. Condition the brush in water before dipping into the paint. Follow the same brush techniques as in Brushing Water-Based Urethane on page 96. When brushing out latex paint, apply it thinly but wet enough to keep a "wet edge." Allow it to dry according to the manufacturer's directions.

Step 7: Clean your brush by swishing in water and ammonia (50/50) and then shampoo with the brush cleaner.

Step 8: Sand with 320-grit abrasive on a block to smooth and level the surface. If the sandpaper loads up, then the paint is still not dry or hard enough (see **Figure 5.34**).

Step 9: Tack off and apply a second coat as pristinely as possible. Clean your brush, allow the second coat to dry, and sand smooth again.

Step 10: The final coat is a clear coat with a water-based product in the sheen of your choice. Follow the procedure for Brushing Water-Based Urethane on page 96 using the same brush you used in that exercise. Apply a thin, uniform coat and then clean the brush. Two coats may be necessary (see **Figure 5.35**).

Step 11: Allow the surface to cure for at least three days. A soft rub-out as described on page 122 will provide a smooth, lustrous surface.

Figure 5.33. Carefully inspect the surface again and fill any remaining imperfections with spackle.

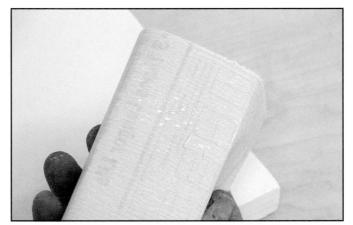

Figure 5.34. If the paper clogs, the paint isn't dry yet.

Figure 5.35. Apply one or two thin coats of clear water-based urethane.

Milk Paint Sample Board

Milk paint is at least as old as Ancient Egypt. The early American settlers used it simply because there were no manufactured paints available until the middle of the 1800s. Many Shaker antiques have an elusive and highly prized original color that is simply good old milk paint mellowed by years of handling and use.

Milk paint is most often used on traditional antique reproductions, but there are contemporary furniture makers who enjoy the subtle variations in color that it provides. When combined with distressing, glazing, and layering multiple colors, the results are pleasing and unique.

When milk paint was made by hand, the painter followed recipes for the colors. Even with recipes, however, variations in pigments and between painters produced variations in color. The pigments that were available came from earth tones: browns (umbers), yellows (ochres), black (lampblack), white (historically lead based), red (iron oxide), and green (from copper). The other ingredients included curdled milk, lime, and chalk or clay as a thickener.

Today, it isn't necessary to use "ol' timey" recipes; numerous companies make traditional milk paint (see Product Sources on page 188 for more information). The consistency of these products, sold as a powder and then mixed with water, is great.

Tools and Materials

- Milk paint (such as The Old-Fashioned Milk Paint Co.'s Milk Paint or J. E. Moser's Genuine Old-Fashioned Milk Paint in Salem red and black)
- Panel or scrap of wood (hard or soft), 6" x 8"
- Foam or chip brushes
- Mixing containers and sticks
- Rough cloth (such as terry cloth)
- 2-pound cut, dewaxed shellac (such as Sealcoat)
- Satin or flat clear finish, water- or oil-based
- Warm water
- Scotchbrite or sandpaper

Step 1: Mix the black milk paint by adding approximately equal parts of warm water and powder together. Always add the powder to the water (see **Figure 5.36**). Stir two to three minutes and then allow the paint to sit for 15 minutes or so. It will thicken, so a bit more water may be needed. (If a paint-like consistency is desired, keep the mix on the thick side. If a more wash-like appearance is desired, keep the mix watery.)

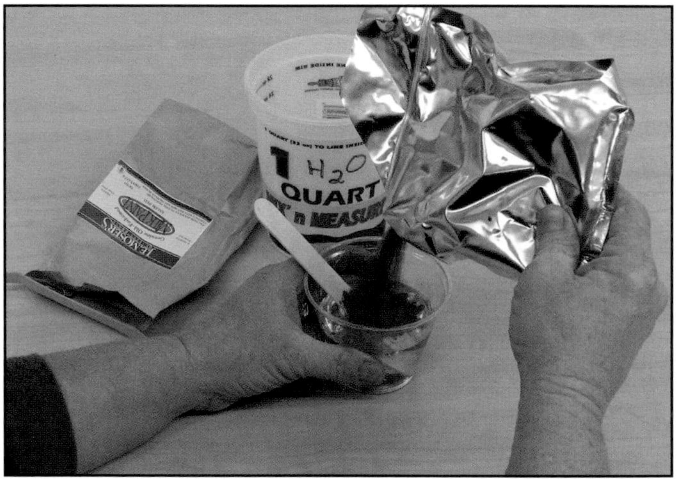

Figure 5.36. Add the milk paint powder to warm water to achieve the consistency of paint.

Helpful Tip _____

Topcoating Milk Paint

Milk paint is a delicate finish but can be topcoated with clear oil-based products to increase durability. Left unprotected, milk paint will water spot. When a topcoat is used, the color deepens in tone. A test sample is critical to avoid disappointments!

Step 2: Apply the black milk paint with a chip or foam brush (see **Figure 5.37**). Be mindful of your brush strokes because the paint holds them when dry.

Step 3: Wait for an hour (or more) and lightly scuff the black. Mix and apply the red on top of the black in long, smooth strokes (see **Figure 5.38**).

Step 4: To allow the black to peek through the red, take a rough cloth (such as terry cloth) that is damp with water and wipe back some of the red (see **Figure 5.39**). You will have an hour or so before the red dries too hard for a damp rag. If it starts to get too difficult, then Scotchbrite or sandpaper will remove the red once it is dry. Keep the removal subtle and light.

Step 5: Seal the surface with shellac. Allow it to dry, scuff lightly, and apply a water- or oil-based clear topcoat.

Step 6: Stand back and admire your work (see **Figure 5.40**)! Now imagine all the other color combinations that are possible through layering and cutting through several colors!

Figure 5.37. Apply milk paint directly to bare wood; don't seal or prime first.

Figure 5.38. Apply the red milk paint over the black.

Figure 5.39. Expose the black by selectively wiping off the wet red.

Figure 5.40. Color effects like this are just the beginning. Milk paint is versatile.

Helpful Tip

Keep Milk Paint Fresh

Milk paint requires frequent stirring during use. Also, keep in mind that it contains milk. If you need to keep it overnight after mixing it with water, store it in the refrigerator to keep it from spoiling. Mix only enough for the project at hand.

Distressed Two-Color Milk Paint Panel

Milk paint is used most frequently on antique reproductions. This exercise includes the distressing commonly applied to such projects. Care, judgment, and restraint will produce attractive reproductions; getting carried away will produce disappointments.

Step 1: Prepare and apply the red paint as described in Milk Paint Sample Board on page 114, right on the raw wood. For a primitive look, don't fill or seal the knots (see **Figure 5.41**). Allow it to dry for an hour or more.

Step 2: Following the instructions that came with it, apply the crackle mixture on top of the red (see **Figure 5.42**). Apply a full coat. If the surface is vertical, be careful about drips and sags. Allow it to dry for 2 hours or more.

Figure 5.41. Apply the paint directly to the wood. By using more water (or less powder) in mixing the milk paint, the wood can show through.

Figure 5.42. Antique crackle will give the next coat of milk paint the shrunken appearance often seen on the finishes of genuine antiques.

Step 3: Apply the black in long strokes without overbrushing. In some instances the black almost immediately crackles, and brushing over it ruins it (see **Figure 5.43**). For large "cracks," use a thicker coat of the black paint. For smaller "cracks," keep the coat thin. Allow the crackled surface to dry thoroughly (usually 2 to 3 hours).

Step 4: Distress the sample board, as shown in **Figures 5.44**, **5.45**, **5.46**, **5.47**, and **5.48**.

Step 5: Lightly smooth the entire board with 320-grit abrasive and tack off. Apply the burnt umber glaze as described in Chapter 4 on page 86 and wipe it off. Let it dry for 4 to 6 hours.

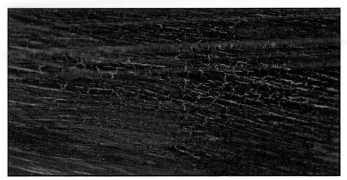

Figure 5.43. The overcoat of black shrinks as it dries giving the "crackle look" of very old finishes.

Figure 5.44. Begin distressing by using the Sureform tool and "wearing" the corners and edges as though this practice panel might be a cabinet door.

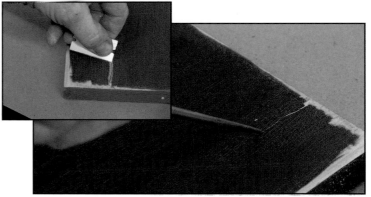

Figure 5.45. Sand the areas roughed up by the Sureform tool with 180- or 220-grit abrasive; then, use the awl to cut in a fake crack, and use a scraper or single-edge razor blade to pull a little of the paint away from the "crack."

Step 6: Seal your primitive panel with a thin coat of shellac. Allow it to dry and topcoat with a low sheen or dead flat oil- or water-based finish. Put a neat old knob on there and you would swear that it looks like an antique (see **Figure 5.49**)!

Figure 5.46. With sandpaper on a block or the Scotchbrite, wear down the black around the knots to reveal wood.

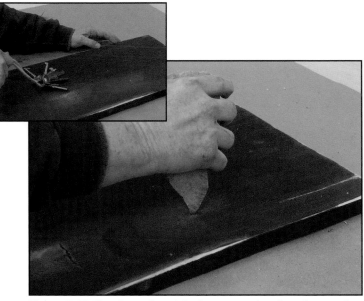

Figure 5.47. Use the rock and the keys to apply a few dings and dents here and there.

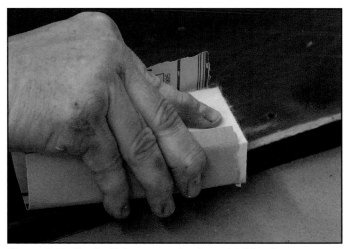

Figure 5.48. Finally, if there was a knob on this "door," wear a spot around it as though worn from daily use.

Figure 5.49. The final result. Use your judgment and apply the techniques to satisfy your own taste.

Helpful Tip _____

Realistic Distressing

Keep the distressing random and sensible.
The most wear on a real piece would be where someone handles the door frequently. Or if it is a cabinet, the hard-hit areas would be nearer the bottom.

More on Painting

Painting can be very exciting. Once the basics outlined here are mastered, you can move on to faux painting, Early American putty or vinegar paint, and grain painting (see **Figure 5.50**). Learn more from the following publications:

• Issue #70 of *American Woodworker* magazine, December 1998, for a recipe for vinegar paint

• *The Art of the Painted Finish*, Isabel O'Neil

• *Paint Magic*, Jocasta Innes

• *American Painted Furniture*, Dean A. Fales, Jr.

Figure 5.50. A lift top, three-drawer, pine blanket chest built and putty painted by the author in the style of an early 1800s chest.

Rubbing out finishes

I mentioned before that rubbing out amounts to finishing the finish. It does more than that. It gives your whole project the look of the master's touch (see **Figure 5.51**). It's inappropriate if your project is a reproduction primitive piece. It's the crowning touch if your project is not a primitive piece. Just as a hand scraper removes the subtle traces of a perfectly honed and tuned smooth plane, rubbing out removes the subtle traces of the brush, which occur even when the brush is handled by a master. Even if you never go beyond brushing varnish on bare wood, learn to rub it out. You'll be glad you did.

Figure 5.51. Finishing a tabletop's smooth surface by rubbing out creates a beautiful light-reflecting polish, as with this antique walnut tabletop.

Covered in this section:

Soft Rub-Out for Penetrating Wipe-On Finishes

The thin topcoat typical of wipe-on finishes lacks the depth needed for a full rub-out but can still benefit from some smoothing out. This "soft" or "simple" rub-out provides it.

> **Tools and Materials**
> - Panel with three to four coats of wipe-on finish, fully cured
> - 0000 steel wool, preferably in a roll
> - Wax or Wool Lube
> - Rags

Step 1: Begin by preparing a panel with at least three or four coats of wipe-on finish such as the panel produced in Wiping On Varnish on page 104. Allow the finish to cure for three to four days, or longer if you can.

Step 2: Cut a 10- to 12-inch section of 0000 steel wool from the roll, and refold it to a flat pad that will fit the flat of your hand. If you are using steel wool pads, unfold the pad and refold it into a shape that fits the length of your hand. Pour a dollop of Wool Lube or scoop a tablespoon of wax into the steel wool (see **Figure 5.52**).

Step 3: Begin rubbing with the grain using long strokes and firm pressure (see **Figure 5.53**). Keep the steel wool lubricated, and don't roll over any edges or you will rub right through the finish. For surfaces that aren't flat, form a matching shape of steel wool to rub out those areas. Buff off the Wool Lube or wax with a soft rag. The result is a "brushed steel" appearance, a satin finish.

Figure 5.52. Wool Lube and steel wool, together, produce a soft rub-out.

Figure 5.53. Long strokes and firm pressure produce the best results.

Adventures in Finishing

Once you rub out your finish, you will, of course, want to give your piece proper care, unlike the unscrupulous antique dealer named Andre in this story:

One day Andre bought a beautiful cabinet with bronze inlay all over it. He was a real wheeler-dealer, and with a few calls he had it sold before he even made it home. He just had to deliver it the next day. Being a haphazard sort, Andre's usual transportation was the open pickup and tarp method, and this day wasn't any different. The cabinet came home open-air style. Needing a beer badly, Andre went into the house and promptly forgot that the cabinet was in the back of the truck. You know, of course, that it rained. You also know that the tarp was on there rather haphazardly, typical of Andre. So the next morning he discovered, to his horror, that a portion of the cabinet was drenched. Not only that, the blowing tarp whipping around had popped out much of the bronze inlay and was missing. He panicked. What to do? It was already sold. Andre went into his garage and searched for anything that would work. He came across some metal powders that were in a box-lot from an auction and began to think. How can these metals be glued into the tiny areas where the inlay was missing? Ah hah! Mix them into some epoxy and pour them into the spots. And that is exactly what Andre did, and it fooled the buyer, for a while. How do I know this story? I was the one who bought the cabinet from Andre! I had to rework that fixit job a little, but it really wasn't bad.

Helpful Tip _____

Rub Out in Proper Order
The fine scratches of a soft rub-out have a definite direction that should follow the grain. Rub out rails first, then stiles, because it's easier to control the edge of the rubbing than the end. By rubbing out the stiles last, you can obliterate any overshoot from the rails onto the stiles.

Helpful Tip _____

Dealing with Wipe-On Finish Build-Up
If a wipe-on finish has been built up to a substantial film thickness, start with a light scuff sanding to remove some of the bumps and lumps. Then, rub out with steel wool.

Full Rub-Out for Brush-On Finishes

Even flawless brushing techniques leave a "just been finished" look, which can be very brassy. A rub-out smoothes out the brush strokes, dust nibs, and heavy spots to an even sheen, either satin or high gloss.

A successful rub-out depends on three conditions:

1. **Choice of sheen.** If multiple coats of a satin finish have been applied, the end result can never be a true high gloss. Some finishers simply use gloss all the time and rub to the desired sheen. This allows better clarity for the finished surface.

2. **Cure time.** Almost all finishes require 200 hours (or more) to reach full cure under optimum conditions. (That's not a misprint. It's eight days and nine nights.) If an oil finish has been applied and allowed to dry at 50 degrees, it might take several weeks. Rubbing out a green finish is like polishing Jell-O. It's too soft to abrade with the fine abrasives used in polishing.

3. **Film thickness.** The project must have five to seven coats applied properly, as described in Brush-On Topcoats on page 92. Just before the final coat or two, level and remove all of the brush strokes, sags, drips, and dust nibs built up from the previous coats. If there isn't enough finish, the risk of cutting through is very high. If in doubt, add more coats.

Tools and Materials

- Panel with five to seven coats of brush-on finish, fully cured
- Mineral spirits
- Paraffin oil
- Spritzer bottles
- Pumice
- Rottenstone
- 2 large saltshakers
- Wet/dry abrasive paper in grits of 400, 600, 800, 1000, 1500 and 2000 (see the sidebar Grit Grades on page 159)
- Firm sanding block
- 2 new felt blocks
- Rags
- Paste wax
- Permanent marker
- Good backlighting
- Saucer
- Horsehair brush
- Dry abrasive

Step 1: Prepare a panel with at least five to seven coats of brush-on finish such as oil-based urethane. Allow the finish to cure for at least 200 hours at room temperature, or longer if you can.

Step 2: Prepare the lubricant by mixing one part mineral spirits and one part oil in a spritzer bottle. Pour the pumice and rottenstone into large saltshakers for ease of application. Mark one with a P and the other with an R.

Figure 5.54. Long, flat strokes with the grain produce the best result.

Step 3: Level the surface of the panel. An almost flawless surface could be leveled by wet sanding with 1000 grit. If the finish has big problems, you might have to start as coarse as 400 grit. Choose the paper, quarter the sheet, and wrap one piece around the block. Spritz the lubricant across the surface and begin wet sanding with long, flat strokes, preferably with the grain (see **Figure 5.54**). Wipe off the slurry frequently to check progress. The goal is to have no shiny spots on the surface. (Shiny spots are low spots in the finish—a few pinhead-size spots are okay).

Step 4: Once level, progress in grit increments of 200 up to 1000 grit. Wipe off the surface thoroughly between grits and after 1000 grit. If your goal is a satin finish, proceed to Step 5/Satin. If your goal is a gloss finish, continue with 1500 grit and 2000 grit and then skip to Step 5/Gloss.

Step 5/Satin: Pour 100% paraffin or mineral oil into another spritzer bottle and spritz the surface; then sprinkle with pumice (see **Figure 5.55**). Mark a new felt block P for pumice with a permanent marker pen. Never use this block with anything but pumice. Squirt plenty of oil into the block to "warm it up." Once the block becomes saturated with oil and pumice, it will be good for a lifetime. (Store it in a baggie.) Begin rubbing with the block, blending the pumice and oil together to create an abrasive gravy. Add oil and pumice if it gets too dry. Long strokes with the grain will produce a satin sheen on the surface. When first learning this process, wipe the slurry off frequently to check progress. The goal is a consistent, long scratch pattern that reminds you of brushed steel. Any errant scratches that go off into left field need further rubbing. When you are satisfied with the scratch pattern and sheen, stop. This is a satin sheen (see **Figure 5.56**).

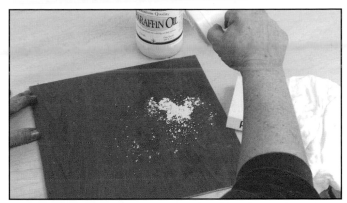

Figure 5.55. Spritz the surface with a fine film of oil and sprinkle with pumice.

Figure 5.56. This is a satin, or "pumice," finish.

Helpful Tip

Choose your Lubricant Carefully

Water, with or without soap, is a lubricant (see **Figure 5.57**) but is extremely aggressive. **Never use water when wet sanding shellac.**

One-hundred percent mineral spirits is less aggressive than water but more aggressive than oil. It can soften some water-based coatings.

Pure mineral, baby, or paraffin oil (all interchangeable) are good but slow.

A mixture of one of the oils and mineral spirits is a good compromise for all rub-outs.

Wax is good but slow. If you cut through, all wax has to be removed before repairing the damage by recoating.

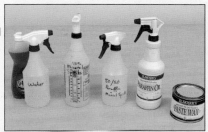

Figure 5.57. Several lubricants are possible but behave differently. Choose carefully.

Step 5/Gloss: You can achieve a full-blown gloss only if you began with a practice panel with four to seven coats of gloss finish. Mark a new felt block R for rottenstone with a permanent marker pen. Never use this block with anything but rottenstone. Pour 100% paraffin or mineral oil into a spritzer bottle and spritz the surface with a fine film of oil. Sprinkle the panel with rottenstone (see **Figure 5.58**). Prime the new felt block with oil, and begin rubbing with the grain in long strokes and with moderate pressure. Keep the surface and the block moist with oil. Wipe off frequently and check your progress in good backlighting. The goal is a flawless, scratch-free, glossy surface. When you've reached that goal, remove all of the oil sludge thoroughly with clean, dry rags. You can now buff out the surface with paste wax (see **Figure 5.59**).

Step 6: For real projects with non-flat surfaces, mix a slurry of oil and abrasive powder in a saucer, wrap a rag around your finger, and dip into it. Rub the areas until the sheen approximates the sheen on the flat panel. Areas that have deep recesses can be "rubbed," so to speak, by brushing into them with a horsehair brush and dry abrasive.

Figure 5.58. A rub-out with rottenstone will produce a high gloss.

Figure 5.59. A beautiful high gloss receiving an application of wax.

Helpful Tip _____

Substitutes for Paste Wax

Modern auto-finish products such as 3M Perfect-It, Meguier's Swirl Remover, or Trans Star Tri-Cut are excellent as a substitute for the paste wax in cleaning up any tiny scratches and will provide a super luster.

Grit Grades

When is a 600 grit not a 600 grit? The American CAMI system of grading abrasive grits was once the only system found in this country. Now abrasives graded with the European "P" system are co-mingling with the CAMI system abrasives on store shelves and are not always clearly marked. A CAMI 600 grit is comparable to a P1200. If you're accustomed to the CAMI system and pick up a "600" that happens to be P600, you've picked up an abrasive comparable to a little more than a CAMI 320. That could be disastrous if you mean to level with CAMI 600- and are actually using the equivalent of CAMI 360-grit. Look on the back of the paper you are using for the grading system. If it doesn't tell you what grading system it's marked with, ask the distributor or the manufacturer. The following table, Grit Grading Systems Compared, outlines the similarities and differences of the different grading systems.

Grit Grading Systems Compared

USA CAMI Grade	European "P" Grade	Coarseness Rating
2000		
1500		Micro Fine
1200		Micro Fine
1000		Micro Fine
800		Ultra Fine
600	P1200	Ultra Fine
500	P1000	Ultra Fine
400	P800	Super Fine
360	P600	Super Fine
320	P500	Extra Fine
280	P400	Extra Fine
240	P280	Very Fine
220	P220	Very Fine
180	P180	Very Fine
150	P150	Very Fine
120	P120	Fine
100	P100	Fine
80	P80	Medium
60	P60	Medium
50	P50	Coarse
40	P40	Coarse
36	P36	Extra Coarse
30	P30	Extra Coarse
24	P24	Extra Coarse
20	P20	Extra Coarse
16	P16	Extra Coarse
12	P12	Extra Coarse

High-Tech Rub-Out

You can take the elbow grease out of a rub-out with a random orbit sander, saving an immense amount of time, especially for large, flat surfaces. The process follows the same order as the hand method. Make sure that the backup pad on your sander is very flat (see **Figure 5.60**). Buy a new replacement pad if needed.

Step 1: Put the 1000-grit disc on the random orbit sander and plug it into a GFI outlet. (This provides a measure of safety against shock when using the lubricant.) Spritz the surface with the lubricant and begin leveling, moving the sander across the surface. Do not bear down on the sander. Wipe the surface frequently to check your progress. The goal is to have very few shiny spots.

Step 2: Switch to a 1500-grit disc and keep leveling with lubricant. Stop when there are no shiny spots left on the panel. Wipe the panel clean of all lubricant.

Step 3: Switch to the Abralon 2000-grit pad. Use the same lubricant and allow the sander to float across the panel. It doesn't matter what direction you move the sander (see **Figure 5.61**). Wipe off the lubricant after two to three minutes to check your progress. Use backlighting to see how the panel is reflecting. There should be an even satin sheen with no apparent scratch pattern. This is an ideal satin sheen. If you look very closely or under magnification, you will see a random set of swirls. Unlike the steel wool method, which left long scratches, this method produces a nearly flawless satin sheen, at least to the naked eye.

Step 4: If the goal is a high gloss, then switch to Abralon 4000 grit. Using the lubricant, float the sander across the panel. Periodically check your progress in the backlighting until the panel is nearly flawless. The scratch pattern should be almost undetectable to the naked eye.

Tools and Materials

- Random orbit sander with a hook and loop pad
- Access to a GFI outlet
- Good backlighting
- Practice panel with four to seven coats of gloss built up and fully cured
- Mirka Royal micro discs in 1000 and 1500 grit
- Mirka Abralon pads in 2000 and 4000 grit
- Oil-and-spirits lubricant for wet sanding
- Clean rags
- Swirl remover (such as Trans Star Tri-Cut)
- Clean rags
- Hand-held buffer

Figure 5.60. You no doubt have the sander; you'll have to get the abrasives.

Helpful Tip _____

What If You Cut Through the Finish while Rubbing-Out?

There is always a risk of cutting through the finish during the rub-out process. If you do, stop, clean off the lubricant thoroughly, and recoat with the same finish. It's possible to recoat just the problem area and feather out the overlap at the edges, but when you are new at this, it may be easier to just recoat the entire surface. Allow it to cure, and then continue with the rub-out schedule. If color is also missing where you cut through, refer to the exercises on repairing and touch up on pages 164 to 173.

Step 5: To achieve the "wet look" and to deal with the minute swirls, the next product is the TriCut Swirl Remover. On small projects, it can be used by hand, but a dining room tabletop should be finished off with a hand-held buffer. Squeeze a small amount of the product onto a clean, soft rag. Begin rubbing it on with moderate pressure. As it dries, buff out with a different soft cloth until the powdery residue is gone and your smiling face is reflected back at you (see **Figure 5.62**)! You have now graduated into the realm of professional finishers! Everyone will feel the fine, rubbed-out surface on your project and ooh and aah all over it. You can take a well-deserved bow.

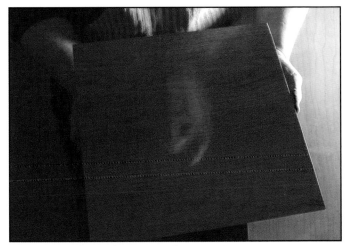

Figure 5.61. This panel has a 2000-grit or satin sheen.

Helpful Tip _____

Rubbing Out Urethane or Varnish

If you are rubbing out a urethane or a varnish (water or oil based), the success of the rub-out is dependant upon the thorough leveling you did prior to the last one to two coats. If no leveling was done then, you will cut through the layers of urethane and create "witness" lines when you level here. If this happens, there's nothing to be done but stop, recoat, and let it cure.

Want to know more about witness lines? Check out Bob Flexner's book *Understanding Wood Finishing*.

Figure 5.62. This is gloss, as good as it gets!

Adventures in Finishing

The process of rubbing out a finish has a definite meditative quality to it. Just ask one student of mine who could have been a Buddhist . . .

The week-long workshop that I teach always ends on a high note by rubbing out panels to perfection. I was particularly fond of one group of students because they were definitely "grooving" on the whole finishing thing. One gentleman, Rob, who tended to be on the quiet side, began his pumice procedure amidst the clatter and chatter of the other students. Everyone else was progressing nicely through the pumice and rolled into the rottenstone . . . except for Rob. Deliberately, and almost in a trancelike state, he kept rubbing and rubbing with the same pumice block. Occasionally adding oil but no additional pumice, he was still at it when most of the others were well into the rottenstone. Finally, when it was killing me, I asked Rob how (and what) he was doing. He smiled and handed me his panel. It was a thing of joy, a panel of perfection, an almost flawless gloss, and with just the pumice! Everyone came over to look at this phenomenon and asked how it was possible. I explained that pumice is a very finely ground lava and breaks down as it is being used. Rob simply broke it down to an ever-finer polishing abrasive. It was a learning experience for the teacher as well—I seem to always learn from my students!

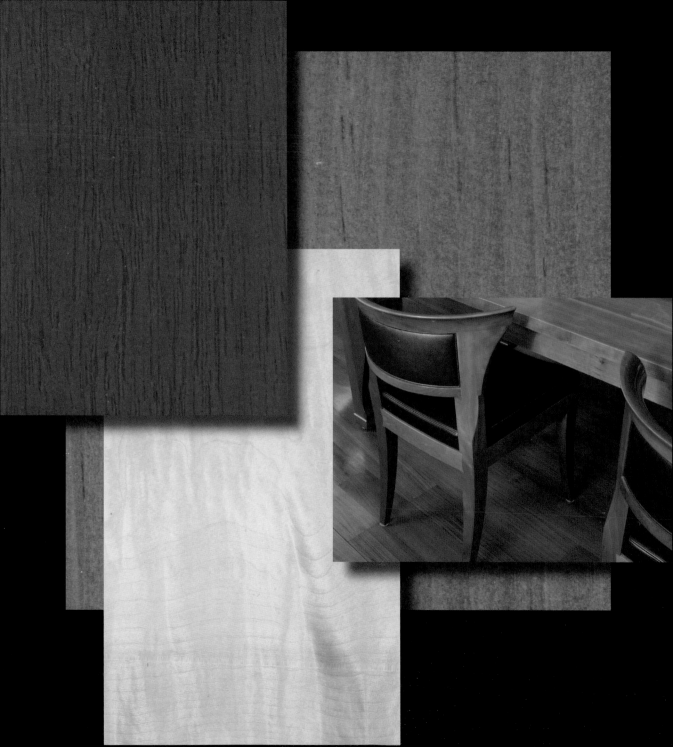

FINISHING RECIPES

· ·

The recipes provided here tell you the specific products and the
sequence of applying them used to achieve the results shown in the
accompanying photos. For more detailed application instructions, see
the relevant exercises in the earlier chapters. As you gain experience and
develop your own recipes, keep a record of the product and sequence
information along with your own notes and the test sample showing
the results. The more recipes you develop, the easier it will be to forget
important details.

The first section of this chapter, Frequently Used Recipes, gives
recipes for the most popular final results and includes abbreviated
application instructions that assume familiarity with the techniques
explained in previous chapters. They will provide a bridge for those with
limited experience.

You will find many more test samples and their ingredients but without specific instructions in the second section of this chapter, A Gallery
of Glorious Woods and Colors, beginning on page 150. These are
intended to stimulate the imagination of more experienced finishers.

Frequently used recipes

Take advantage of this section by using and expanding my recipes to your own benefit. The specific recipes here are ones I use all the time and ones that I teach in my finishing classes. Remember, any formulas must be written down and saved in the recipe box (see **Figure 6.1**).

Figure 6.1. Use a recipe box to store the recipes for all your favorite finishing concoctions.

Tools and Materials
- Scraps of wood
- Your favorite colors
- Documentation
- Imagination

Covered in this section:

Cherry

page 134

Highly Figured Wood

page 142

Walnut

page 136

Pine

page 144

Oak

page 138

"Secret" Wiping Varnish Recipes

page 146

Mahogany

page 140

Mixing your Own Shellac from Flakes

page 148

Cherry

Cherry is a difficult wood to color because of its tendency to blotch. Here are a few of my recipes to avoid the problem.

Cherry #1: Blending cherry sapwood

Step 1: Wash coat just the pink heartwood right up to the white sapwood (see **Figure 6.2**). The color that you need to mimic is the wash-coated pink heartwood.

Step2 : Prepare the tinted wash coat for the white sapwood by blending powdered pigments into a wash coat on a piece of glass. Try Behlen cherry and light walnut or Homestead burnt umber and burnt sienna. Keep it "wash" consistency, *not* like paint. Test it on the wood, and then lightly color in the white streak, drawing the brush full of color down the line between the pink and the white without overlapping onto the pink (see **Figure 6.3**).

Step 3: If you like, you can further disguise the sapwood by scuffing with 320 grit and then glazing the entire surface (see **Figure 6.4**). Wash coat before topcoating.

Figure 6.2. Wash coat the heartwood with untinted shellac wash coat.

Figure 6.3. Wash coat the sapwood with a carefully tinted shellac wash coat.

Figure 6.4. A glaze will further hide the sapwood.

Cherry #2: A deep antique cherry

Step 1: Stain the cherry with Clearwater Smooth and Simple antique cherry. Allow it to dry for 6 to 8 hours.

Step 2: Stain right over the first stain with Bartley's Pennsylvania cherry. Allow it to dry for 6 to 8 hours and then topcoat (see **Figure 6.5**).

Figure 6.5. Stain over stain produces unique results.

Cherry #3: Mimicking cherry with poplar or alder

Step 1: Wash coat with glue size to minimize stain absorption.

Step 2: Stain with Mohawk light golden oak. Allow it to dry for 8 hours.

Step 3: Wash coat and scuff with 320 grit, and then glaze with Behlen's burnt umber Shading and Glazing stain (see **Figure 6.6**). Wipe off gently and allow it to dry for 6 hours. Wash coat. Additional glazes can be added for further color before topcoating.

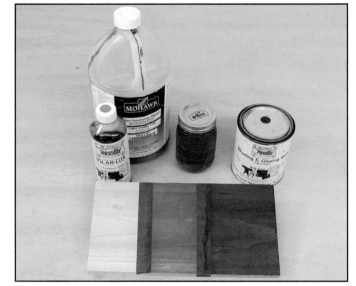

Figure 6.6. A step sample shows the progression: wash coat, stain, and glaze.

Walnut

Walnut is a beautiful wood that can be very rich and lustrous when finished with color. Simply oiling it and leaving it natural cheats it out of an opportunity for incredible beauty.

Walnut #1: Blending walnut sapwood

Step 1: Blend walnut sapwood to match the heartwood following the steps in the recipe for cherry sapwood on page 134, but choose the pigments carefully (see **Figure 6.7**). Some walnut has a purple tint to it, so mix your colors accordingly.

Figure 6.7. Blend walnut sapwood using the same techniques as blending cherry sapwood.

Walnut #2: A rich antique walnut

Step 1: Stain the walnut with Solar-Lux lemon yellow dye. Allow to dry 6 to 8 hours, wash coat, and scuff.

Step 2: Glaze with Behlen's burnt umber glaze. Allow it to dry for 6 hours.

Step 3: Wash coat and scuff with 320 grit.

Step 4: Glaze with Mohawk dark mahogany glaze (see **Figure 6.8**). Allow to dry 6 hours and wash coat, then topcoat (see **Figure 6.9**).

Figure 6.8. The five steps: stain, wash coat, glaze, wash coat, and another glaze.

Figure 6.9. This recipe works stunningly well on a fine piece of crotch walnut.

Oak

Everyone has different ideas on what color oak should be. Here are four
recipes that hit most flavors from light to very dark.

Oak #1: Rich caramel brown

Step 1: Stain with Smooth And Simple antique cherry, dry for 8 hours, wash coat, and then scuff with 320 grit.

Step 2: Glaze with Behlen's raw umber, dry 6 hours,
wash coat, and then topcoat (see **Figure 6.10**).

Figure 6.10. A cherry stain and a raw umber glaze produce this
deep, warm result.

Oak #2: Deep brown fumed oak

Step 1: Stain with Clearwater Smooth And Simple mission oak, dry 6 to 8 hours, wash coat, and then scuff with 320 grit.

Step 2: Glaze with Behlen's burnt umber glaze (for a deeper brown, mix some black glaze into the burnt umber), wash coat when dry, and then topcoat (see **Figure 6.11**). When the finish is totally cured, a black wax can be used to further accentuate the grain.

Figure 6.11. Just one stain and one glaze produce these beautiful colors.

Oak #3: A nice brown oak

Step 1: Dye the oak with Mohawk light golden oak (or Solar-Lux golden fruitwood). Allow it to dry for 8 hours.

Step 2: Apply medium walnut Danish oil (or tint a clear Danish oil to a color you prefer with one of the Woodburst colors) (see **Figure 6.12**). Add several more coats of oil to build an adequate topcoat.

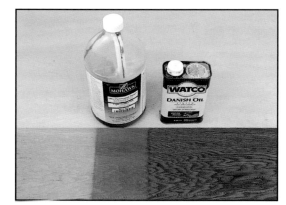

Figure 6.12. A stain and then a colored oil produce rich colors if you prefer a simple medium tone.

Oak #4: An unusual oak color

Step 1: Dye the oak with Solar-Lux bright red, allow to dry, wash coat, and then scuff.

Step 2: Glaze with Behlen's black glaze, wash coat, and then topcoat (see **Figure 6.13**).

Figure 6.13. It takes a strong glaze color to affect such a brilliant base color, but the result can be stunning.

Mahogany

When I think of mahogany, it's usually an antique color, but here are some variations that are very beautiful. The only recipe you won't see is the "blond" mahogany from the 1960s.

Mahogany #1: A pleasant nut-brown mahogany

Step 1: Wash coat the mahogany, allow it to dry, and then scuff.

Step 2: Glaze with Behlen's burnt umber, wash coat after 6 hours, and then topcoat (see **Figure 6.14**).

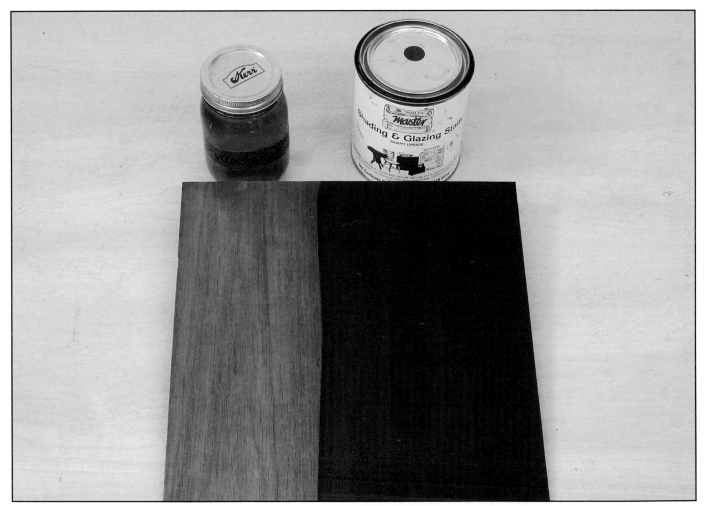

Figure 6.14. Often, a single application of color produces the desired effect.

Mahogany #2: A deep antique mahogany

Step 1: Stain with Solar-Lux lemon yellow, dry for 8 hours, wash coat, and then scuff with 320-grit.

Step 2: Apply grain filler tinted with burnt umber Japan color, allow it to dry, and then wash coat.

Step 3: Glaze with Mohawk dark mahogany, dry for 6 hours, and then wash coat.

Step 4: Glaze with Behlen's van dyke tinted to your liking with Behlen's black glaze. Wash coat when dry; then, topcoat with a full film finish and polish out when cured (see **Figure 6.15**).

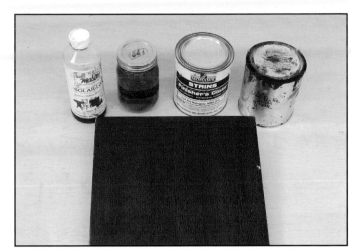

Figure 6.15. In this sample, a total of five products combine to produce the desired result. (The fifth product is the grain filler, which is not shown.)

Mahogany #3: A deep red "'50s pineapple poster bed" mahogany

Step 1: Stain with Solar-Lux nutmeg brown (or deep red mahogany), dry for 8 hours, wash coat, and then scuff.

Step 2: Apply grain filler tinted with red and van dyke Japan colors, dry, wash coat, and then scuff.

Step 3: Glaze with Mohawk dark mahogany, dry for 6 hours, wash coat, and then scuff.

Step 4: Glaze with Sherwin Williams van dyke (or mix Behlen's van dyke with black), dry, wash coat, and then scuff (see **Figure 6.16**).

Step 5: Apply multiple topcoats and follow a full rub-out schedule.

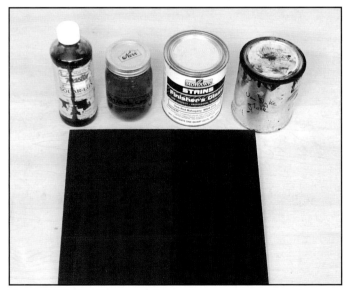

Figure 6.16. Creating a *very* deep color on new wood can be complex and time consuming.

Highly Figured Wood

There is nothing more exciting in finishing than when a piece of tiger or bird's-eye maple comes alive and "dances" in the light. Here are the methods to get there.

Figured Wood #1: The natural effect (tiger maple)

Step 1: Apply two coats of Danish oil thinned 50/50 with mineral spirits then additional full-strength coats to build a topcoat. The oil "blotches" the figure in an attractive way (see **Figure 6.17**).

Figure 6.17. When figure in wood reflects different grain direction, a deeply penetrating finish will emphasize it.

Figured Wood #2: Colored oil (bird's-eye maple)

Step 1: Apply two coats of colored Danish oil thinned 50/50 with mineral spirits then additional full-strength coats to build a topcoat (see **Figure 6.18**). (You can also tint natural Danish oil with Woodburst colors such as cherry.)

Figure 6.18. You can use colored oil in the same simple process as the previous exercise.

Figured Wood #3: Coloring *and* popping the figure (tiger maple)

Step 1: Stain with light golden oak (or golden fruitwood non-grain-raising) and let dry for 6 hours.

Step 2: Apply Danish oil thinned 50/50 with mineral spirits right over the dye stain (see **Figure 6.19**). Allow it to dry for 12 hours and apply a full film finish.

Figure 6.19. A dye stain doesn't seal the wood, allowing a subsequent application of diluted oil to emphasize the grain.

Figured Wood #4: Coloring deeply and sanding back (bird's-eye maple)

Step 1: Stain with a water-based amber dye (or dark brown, or even black), let it dry for 6 hours.

Step 2: Sand with 180 grit to "clean" the upper wood, leaving the colorant in the stripes or "eyes" of the maple (see **Figure 6.20**). This recipe is very labor intensive for non-flat surfaces!

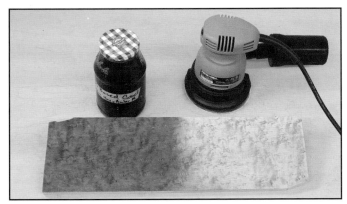

Figure 6.20. When color penetrates in parts of the wood but remains on the surface in other parts, you can emphasize the difference by sanding off the surface color.

Figured Wood #5: Antique maple (bird's-eye maple)

Step 1: Stain with a water-based honey amber dye (either Trans Tint or Moser's powdered dye). Allow it to dry for 6 hours, wash coat, and then scuff with 320 grit.

Step 2: Glaze with Behlen's burnt umber. Allow it to dry for 6 hours, wash coat, and then scuff with 320 grit.

Step 3: Glaze with Behlen's raw umber, leaving it heavy in any molding profiles or turnings. Allow it to dry for 6 hours, wash coat, and then scuff with 320 grit.

Step 4: Topcoat with a low sheen to achieve a realistic antique look (see **Figure 6.21**).

Figure 6.21. Bird's-eye maple with a fine antique appearance.

Pine

Take care with pine—it is a difficult wood to finish! Here are two methods to make pine beautiful.

Pine #1: A light golden pine

Step 1: Wash coat and then scuff with 320 grit.

Step 2: Mix one part Behlen's burnt umber glaze with two parts raw sienna glaze, apply, and allow it to dry for 6 hours.

Step 3: Wash coat, scuff with 320 grit, and then topcoat (see **Figure 6.22**).

Figure 6.22. Glazes over a wash coat produce good color without blotchiness in pine.

Pine #2: Antique pine or fir

Step 1: Sand smooth and remove all dust.

Step 2: Equip a propane torch with a flame spreader as used for roofing or burning weeds.

Step 3: Lay out the boards on a concrete surface away from any combustible materials.

Step 4: Ignite the torch and pass the flame across the wood about 8 to 12 inches away. The goal is to toast the wood to a nice brown color. If you hold the torch too close or if you let the flame rest for a moment, it will burn the spot black. If you hold it too far away or move too fast, you will warm the wood but not toast it (see **Figure 6.23**).

Step 5: Lightly dewhisker the wood with fine Scotchbrite (see **Figure 6.24**).

Step 6: Mix one ounce of Solar-Lux yellow maple dye and one ounce of Mohawk light golden oak dye with a quart of wash coat, and apply it to the toasted wood.

Step 7: Scuff, and then glaze with Behlen's raw umber.

Step 8: Seal with untinted Sealcoat, allow to dry, and topcoat with a satin or flat sheen finish. The finished wood has a beautiful vintage appearance (see **Figure 6.25**)!

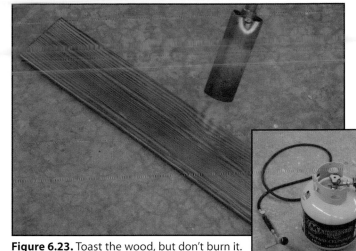

Figure 6.23. Toast the wood, but don't burn it.

Figure 6.24. Smooth the toasted wood with an abrasive pad.

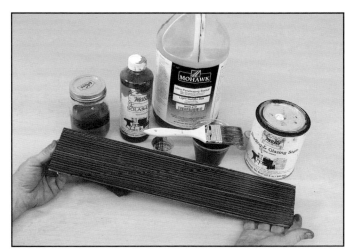

Figure 6.25. The final result: rich and aged.

"Secret" Wiping Varnish Recipes

Every woodworking school in the country has its own formula for a wipe-on oil that students can slather onto their projects. Here are just a few.

Secret #1: From an unnamed school in Maine

Step 1: Use a paint store mixing container with graduations marked on the side.

Step 2: Add one part tung oil.

Step 3: Add one part Waterlox.

Step 4: Add one part mineral spirits.

Step 5: Mix well and apply as a wipe-on finish (see **Figure 6.26**).

Figure 6.26. A simple finish that creates greater durability with six to eight coats. When cured, use the soft rub-out method on page 122.

Secret #2: From an unidentified source

Step 1: Use a paint store mixing container with graduations marked on the side.

Step 2: Add one part boiled linseed or tung oil.

Step 3: Add one part Waterlox XL88 (or McCloskey's Heirloom Varnish) (see **Figure 6.27**).

Step 4: Add one part mineral spirits.

Step 5: Mix well and apply as a wipe-on finish.

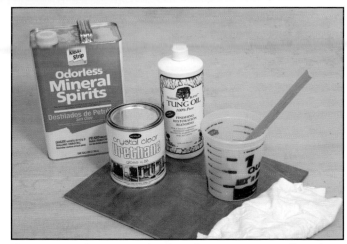

Figure 6.27. When mixing this formula, you are essentially making your own wipe-on polyurethane. Add one part Waterlox gloss urethane (XL88) or McCloskey's Heirloom Varnish.

Secret #3: From an unnamed school in Connecticut

Step 1: A procedure, rather than a formula, for applying wiping varnish: Slather the project generously and re-slather any dry spots for 30 minutes or so, and then wipe off any excess.

Step 2: Every day for three to four days, rub additional wiping varnish into the wood with 4/0 steel wool, and then wipe off any excess.

Step 3: For a higher gloss, apply small amounts of the wiping varnish with a tight wad of cloth such as is used for padding on shellac. Rub it in until the surface is free of excess wet oil, and do not wipe the surface (see **Figure 6.28**).

Figure 6.28. This method is more work, but what a soft silky finish!

Mixing your Own Shellac from Flakes

The proportion of shellac flakes to denatured alcohol is called the "cut." One pound of flakes in one gallon of denatured alcohol is a "1-pound cut." Two pounds of flakes in one gallon of alcohol is a "2-pound cut" and so on. To mix a small amount, simply reduce the ratio. A quarter-pound of flakes in a quart of alcohol will give you a 1-pound cut.

Shellac recipe

Step 1: Weigh out the shellac when mixing for the first time, and then you can eyeball it in the future.

Step 2: Use a glass jar with a lid. Mix the flakes and alcohol by shaking them up (see **Figure 6.29**).

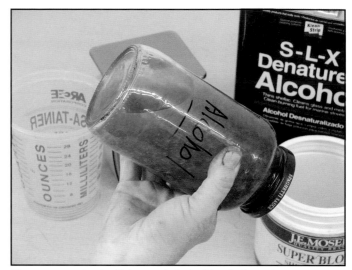

Figure 6.29. Mix the flakes and alcohol by shaking them in a glass jar.

Helpful Tip _____

Padding Lacquers vs. Shellac
Padding lacquers are on the market and can be substituted for the shellac. However, the solvents are stronger, and they have a lubricant added to them for ease of application. Shellac smells better and is less expensive. French polishing is the ultimate in final finishing with shellac, but that is beyond the scope of this book's basic finishing exercises.

Step 3: Continue to shake every so often to keep the flakes from congealing into a thick lump in the bottom of the jar. Usually the shellac is ready to go after 12 hours.

Step 4: There are some flakes that don't dissolve no matter how long they are left. It is best to strain the material through a fine paint filter before use (see **Figure 6.30**).

Figure 6.30. Strain out any residue that won't dissolve.

Helpful Tip

Using Dewaxed Shellac

Wax is a naturally occurring component in shellac, but it interferes with adhesion of other types of finish. If it's going to be used under another finish, it must be free of wax. (Of course if the shellac is going to be used as a finish on its own, this is irrelevant.) Some grades of shellac flakes are dewaxed (others are not), but the company that you bought them from may not know. By mixing your own, you will know because the wax will swirl around in clouds in the jar. Let the solution sit for a few days to settle out (see **Figure 6.31**); then ladle or pour off the clear liquid from the top, and you will have dewaxed shellac.

Figure 6.31. Wax will appear as clouds in the jar. Let the mixture settle and pour out the clear liquid on top to get dewaxed shellac.

A gallery of glorious woods and colors

These wood finish test samples show just some of the finishes that you have now learned how to produce. All of the techniques used are explained in the preceding chapters. The specific finishing products and colors used on the samples are listed in order, beginning with the first product applied to the bare wood. Note that in most cases the specifics of the topcoat don't matter as long as it is clear. In those cases where the specifics do make a difference, they are mentioned. As you experiment with products, sequences, and colors, keep careful notes attached to your test samples so that in a few years you will be able to come back and reproduce the same finish.

Covered in this Section:

Red Oak
page 152

Walnut
page 158

Quarter-Sawn White Oak
page 153

Maple
page 159

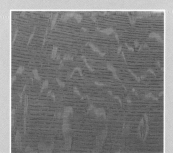

Cherry
page 154

Pine
page 160

Mahogany
page 155

Poplar
page 161

Highly Figured Woods
page 156

Red Oak

Here are four recipes for red oak that can create any tone from light salmon to a dark caramel. Recipe 1 showcases red oak's natural salmon color. Clear coating with a water base accentuates the natural color, whereas oil warms it. Recipe 2 shows that red oak can easily be finished to showcase the simple, crisp color of golden oak. The third recipe might be a two-step formula, but it still easily creates a dark brown color. Recipe 4, a simple stain and glaze combination, brings out the deep caramel brown that antique oak becomes after 100 years.

Red oak with oil-based and water-based topcoats

1 Right side only: Oil-based topcoat.

2 Left side only: Water-based topcoat.

Note how the oil-based finish warms the color of the wood.

Red oak with tinted oil.

Golden oak Danish oil topcoat.

Red oak with stain and oil.

1 Mohawk light golden oak non-grain-raising stain.

2 Medium walnut Danish oil.

3 Topcoat.

Red oak with stain and glaze.

1 Smooth And Simple mission oak stain.

2 Shellac wash coat.

3 Burnt umber and black glaze (mixed).

4 Shellac wash coat.

5 Topcoat.

Quarter-Sawn White Oak

I have included three recipes for quarter-sawn oak: light, medium, and dark. Quarter-sawn white oak comes alive, whether you choose to warm its color with oil or create a deep richness with stain and glaze (see Recipes 1 and 2). Another option is to darken the finish to the popular Mission (or Arts and Crafts) hue, as in Recipe 3.

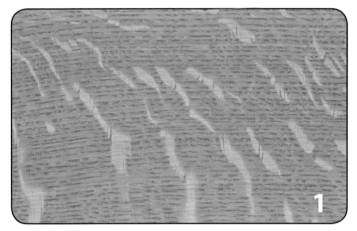

White oak with colored oil.

1 Medium walnut Danish oil.

2 Topcoat.

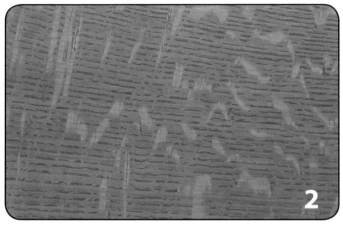

White oak with stain and glaze.

1 Mohawk light golden oak non-grain-raising stain.

2 Shellac wash coat.

3 Burnt umber glaze.

4 Shellac wash coat.

5 Topcoat.

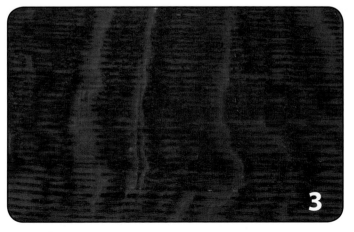

White oak with stain and dark glaze.

1 Smooth And Simple mission oak stain.

2 Shellac wash coat.

3 Burnt umber and black (mixed) glaze.

4 Shellac wash coat.

5 Topcoat.

Cherry

Cherry is a beautiful wood that can be finished to a variety of flattering shades. Finishing with oil (Recipe 1) creates a mild hue, while layering glazes right on top of each other concocts a much darker, richer red color (Recipe 3). Recipe 2 pushes you to think outside the can to achieve a medium red shade (see page 88).

Cherry with Danish oil.

1 Shellac wash coat.

2 Multiple coats of natural Danish oil.

Cherry with glaze.

1 Shellac wash coat.

2 Burnt umber glaze.

3 Shellac wash coat.

4 Topcoat.

Cherry with stain and glaze.

1 Smooth And Simple antique cherry stain.

2 Bartley's Pennsylvania cherry glaze.

3 Topcoat.

Mahogany

Mahogany doesn't have to be limited to its traditional rich color (Recipe 3). Recipe 1 showcases a much lighter side of mahogany that is reached simply with colored oil. Recipe 2 demonstrates the nutmeg brown color created by the ever-faithful burnt umber glaze. To achieve the 1950's pineapple posterbedroom set mahogany hue, try Recipe 4.

Mahogany with colored oil.

1 Medium walnut Danish oil.

2 Topcoat.

Mahogany with glaze.

1 Shellac wash coat.

2 Burnt umber glaze.

3 Shellac wash coat.

4 Topcoat.

Mahogany with stain and glaze.

1 Smooth And Simple antique cherry stain.

2 Shellac wash coat.

3 Burnt umber glaze.

4 Topcoat.

Mahogany with stain and two glazes.

1 Solar-Lux nutmeg brown stain.

2 Shellac wash coat.

3 Mohawk dark mahogany glaze.

4 Shellac wash coat.

5 Sherwin Williams van dyke brown glaze.

6 Shellac wash coat.

7 Topcoat.

Highly Figured Woods

The following six recipes are created to show off highly figured woods like tiger maple and birds' eye maple. Recipe 1 uses Danish oil and mineral spirits to accent the stunning stripes in this tiger maple. Adding color and popping the grain is accomplished with Recipe 3 (see page 143). Recipe 4 utilizes sanding to accentuate the eyes of this birds' eye maple. The perfect recipe for antique reproductions is Recipe 5. Finally, flame birch comes alive when finished with Recipe 6: everyone in my classes thinks of electric guitar bodies when they see this electric red sample!

Emphasizing figured grain. (Tiger maple)

1 Danish oil thinned 50/50 with mineral spirits.

2 Repeat.

3 Topcoat (gloss).

Tinted figured woods. (Bird's-eye maple)

1 Danish oil tinted with Woodburst cherry and thinned 50/50 with mineral spirits.

2 Repeat.

3 Topcoat (gloss).

Figured wood with stain. (Tiger maple)

1 Mohawk light golden oak non-grain-raising stain.

2 Danish oil thinned 50/50 with mineral spirits.

3 Topcoat (gloss).

Figure in wood emphasized by sanding. (Bird's-eye maple)

1 Water-based amber dye.

2 Sand back to "clean" the upper wood.

3 Topcoat.

Figured wood with dye and glaze. (Bird's-eye maple)

1 Honey amber water-based dye.

2 Shellac wash coat.

3 Glaze with burnt umber.

4 Shellac wash coat.

5 Raw umber and black (mixed) glaze.

6 Topcoat.

Figured wood with color. (Flame birch)

1 Solar-Lux bright red stain.

2 Thinned Danish oil.

3 Gloss topcoat.

4 Full rub-out.

Walnut

Although walnut cannot achieve as wide a range of colors as mahogany or oak, the three recipes I've included here bring out the rich natural brown of the wood. Recipe 1 works extremely well on air dried walnut. but if used on kiln dried wood, add a touch of a reddish Danish oil to achieve the same result. Recipe 2 works well for antiques—good ol' burnt umber! I wish there was a way to shorten Recipe 3, but there are no shortcuts to get the dimensional quality of color in this walnut.

Walnut with colored oil.

1 Shellac wash coat.

2 Medium walnut Danish oil.

3 Topcoat.

Walnut with glaze.

1 Shellac wash coat.

2 Burnt umber glaze.

3. Topcoat.

Walnut with stain and two glazes.

1 Solar-Lux lemon yellow stain.

2 Shellac wash coat.

3 Burnt umber glaze.

4 Shellac wash coat.

5 Mohawk dark mahogany glaze.

6 Shellac wash coat.

7 Topcoat.

Maple

These three recipes can transform maple to a pale, warm, or dark shade. The first recipe is a formula for clean, crisp, white maple (with no blotching). Recipe 2 keeps you in control of how much the stain colors the maple. Finally, Recipe 3 transforms the naturally light wood to a dark hue. However, maple is a very difficult wood to darken. You might want to rethink the wood choice in the project if you want a dark color—consider a wood that is already dark, like walnut.

White maple.

1 Shellac wash coat.

2 Water-based topcoat.

Warm maple.

1 Shellac wash coat.

2 Minwax English oak water-based stain.

3 Topcoat.

Maple with stain and glaze.

1 Glue size.

2 Solar-Lux American walnut stain.

3 Shellac wash coat.

4 Sherwin Williams van dyke glaze.

5 Topcoat.

Pine

Pine can be finished to a variety of shades, as shown by these three recipes. Recipe 1 creates a light pine color, but make sure to sand your wood up to 220 when using this recipe. The light color shows everything! In Recipe 2, the gel stain goes right on the bare wood. If you are unwilling to risk blotching, use a washcoat or the gel varnish first, as on page 46. Recipe 3 is an extended version of the conditioning exercise on pages 44 and 45; use it to achieve a rich honey brown color.

Light pine.

1 Shellac wash coat.

2 Minwax English oak water-based stain.

3 Topcoat.

Medium brown pine.

1 Bartley's golden oak stain.

2 Topcoat.

Pine with stain and glaze.

1 Shellac wash coat.

2 Minwax red mahogany stain.

3 Shellac wash coat.

4 Burnt umber glaze.

5 Wash coat.

6 Topcoat.

Poplar

These three recipes showcase a variety of colors that would work for both poplar and alder. Recipe 1 is extremely simple. However, poplar with just a clear top coat isn't very attractive, as the green streaks in the wood show through. Over time, everything will turn more yellow. I like the color that the two glaze colors mix into in Recipe 2. They make poplar look so much better! Recipe 3 is for mimicking cherry when all you have is poplar (or alder).

Poplar au naturel.

1 Clear topcoat (not recommended).

Poplar with mixed glazes.

1 Shellac wash coat.

2 Burnt umber and raw sienna (mixed) glaze.

3 Shellac wash coat.

4 Topcoat.

Poplar with stain and glaze.

1 Glue size.

2 Mohawk light golden oak stain.

3 Shellac wash coat.

4 Raw umber glaze.

5 Shellac wash coat.

6 Topcoat.

REPAIR AND RESTORATION

Maintaining a finish once you've completed a project is as much a part of finishing as the actual application of product. In this chapter, we'll go over a number of exercises for repairing damage, talk about the proper ways to care for your furniture, and look at some methods for assessing and caring for antiques.

Repairing and touching up

Repairing and touching up finishes is a handy skill for either doing your own work or making a handsome living at it working for others. Something always happens when moving a piece of furniture, and few craftsmen know how to fix the damage.

Figure 7.1. Finish repair is hand work. Many materials are available for the job, but few tools are needed.

The number of products on the market for repairing and touching up furniture finishes is huge. Just the products needed for the techniques that follow are extensive, and expensive (see **Figure 7.1**). I am not suggesting that you go out and buy them all. Rather, look over the furniture you already have that needs work, go to the section describing a needed repair that interests you, and get what's needed for that job. If you own a number of antiques, then removing white rings might be useful. Or if your kids have produced a fine haze of scuffs and scratches on your kitchen table, start with polishing out a worn finish.

Most importantly, keep in mind that it's always worth touching up and possibly over-finishing a piece before jumping into the big job of stripping and refinishing. If the touch-up doesn't work out, you have wasted little time, but, if it works, you have saved a lot of time.

Covered in this Section:

Cleaning Off Accumulated Grime

page 166

Filling Larger Holes with Epoxy Putty

page 170

Removing White Rings

page 167

Replacing Color and Over-Finishing

page 171

Filling Small Holes

page 168

Repolishing a Worn Finish

page 172

Filling Larger Holes

page 169

Cleaning Off Accumulated Grime

Before you can even consider what repairs or touching up a finish might require, you need to see the finish clearly, undisguised, not camouflaged by grime that may look like finish. Even if you find nothing wrong, no harm is done. And if you already know there are problems, a good cleaning will tell you how extensive they are and whether there are additional problems that you haven't noticed.

> **Tools and Materials**
> - 0000 (fine) steel wool
> - Wool Lube
> - Mineral spirits
> - Rags

Step 1: Identify and remove the dirt. Take a bit of steel wool with a dollop of Wool Lube and gently scrub an area. Wipe with a rag (see **Figure 7.2**). If the grime comes off, then it's old dirt from normal usage.

Step 2: If steel wool and Wool Lube fail, try mineral spirits. If the spirits take it off, then it's probably a buildup of old waxes and polishes. Keep cleaning. The above two alternatives handle most cases. If neither of them works, try to identify the offending material and select from Cleaners That Work below.

Step 3: Once everything is squeaky clean and dry, examine it carefully. If the finish needs repair, skip to the relevant repair technique in this section. If no repairs are needed and the topcoat is in good condition, just rewax it with a good paste wax. Paste wax is not permanent, and if the wood is grainy, choose a colored wax to blend. Or, you might choose to repolish, or over-finish and repolish, both explained in the following exercises.

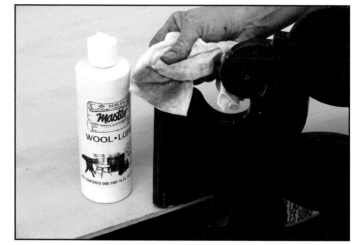

Figure 7.2. Wool Lube and steel wool, followed by a rag, will remove a surprising amount of grime; just look at the rag.

Helpful Tip _____

Cleaners That Work

- *Latex paint spatters* come off with a product like Goof Off, but you can also try the solvent xylene.

- *Magic markers* can be removed with denatured alcohol or lacquer thinner, but be careful to wipe quickly and not with a dripping rag. It could ruin the finish.

- *Crayons* will come right off with mineral spirits.

- *Old stickers and moving tags* can sometimes be lifted by first soaking with vegetable oil. If not, there are products like Un-Du Adhesive Remover on the market that will do the trick. Solvents like mineral spirits or xylene will remove them, but be very careful not to damage the finish.

Removing White Rings

Most white rings occur in finishes that have low resistance to heat, water, or alcohol. The damage may be entirely within the topcoat and be easily repaired, or it may have penetrated all the way to the wood. You won't know until you try to remove it.

Tools and Materials
- Denatured alcohol
- Mineral oil
- Pumice
- Rottenstone
- Rags

Step 1: Try the simplest fix first. Dampen a rag with denatured alcohol and pass over the ring lightly several times. Don't soak the surface. If this method works, it will happen fairly quickly. If nothing happens, move on to Step 2.

Step 2: Try rubbing the spot with oil and pumice as described in Full Rub-Out for Brush-On Finishes, on page 124 (see **Figure 7.3**). If this removes the damage before cutting all the way through the topcoat, it may still leave a sheen different from the rest of the surface. If a rub with rottenstone doesn't eliminate the difference, rub out the entire table surface to whatever sheen you prefer. If you do cut through the topcoat, you may have to replace color (see page 171), and you'll certainly have to apply a new topcoat.

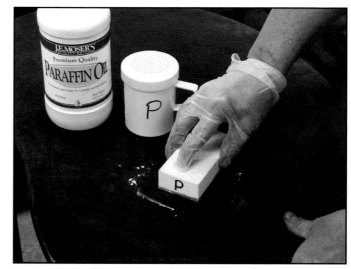

Figure 7.3. Pumice, a fine abrasive, lubricated with mineral oil, will grind out a white ring, but, if the ring goes through to the wood, you'll have to refinish.

Helpful Tip _____

Heat Rings or Water Rings
Rings caused by heat can resemble water rings. Try the two methods on pages 166 and 167. Heat damage may require total refinishing.

Filling Small Holes

The easiest way to make matching repairs to small holes, meaning those smaller than a nail head, is with matching filler. It saves you the hassle of blending colors.

Tools and Materials
- Wax fill sticks
- Aerosol finish of your choice
- Pumice and/or rottenstone

Step 1: Select a matching fill stick, nip off a bit of it, and persuade it into the hole. Blend it in and smooth it with the heat of your finger (see **Figure 7.4**).

Step 2: Protect the fill with a light spritz of an aerosol or a light dot of finish on a brush. Lightly rub out the area to make the repair invisible.

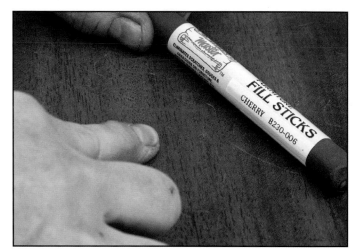

Figure 7.4. Fill sticks are extremely convenient, easy to use, and available in a wide range of colors.

Filling Larger Holes

Fill sticks remain comparatively soft, which isn't a serious problem with small holes. Holes larger than a nail head, however, require a filler with more resistance to deformation in daily use. Burn-in sticks do the trick because it takes much more than finger heat to soften them. You'll need a burn-in knife to apply it.

Tools and Materials
- Burn-in sticks
- Burn-in knife
- 220- or 320-grit abrasive paper
- Firm sanding block
- Oil lubricant

Step 1: Choose a stick that is slightly lighter in color than the undamaged surface.

Step 2: Warm up the burn-in knife well, until it turns the burn-in stick molten when touched. Hold the stick against the knife over the damaged area. Drip the molten burn-in stick into the hole, overfilling it (see **Figure 7.5**).

Step 3: With your finger, tap the warm liquid down to remove air bubbles (see **Figure 7.6**).

Step 4: When the patch has cooled, level very carefully with 220- or 320-grit abrasive paper on a firm block and the oil lubricant (see **Figure 7.7**). Be careful not to sand the surrounding area and damage it. Check for any air bubble holes and refill with more burn-in stick if necessary.

Step 5: When the patch is level and free of bubbles, color and over-finish as described on page 171 (see **Figure 7.8**).

Figure 7.5. Melt the burn-in stick with the burn-in knife, and drip it into the damage.

Figure 7.6. Tap it in with your finger, removing air bubbles.

Figure 7.7. Carefully sand it flush with a fine abrasive.

Figure 7.8. Finally, touch up the color and over-finish.

Filling Larger Holes with Epoxy Putty

A burn-in knife and an assortment of sticks may represent more of an investment than you can justify for occasional use. Epoxy putty is an economical alternative.

Tools and Materials
- Epoxy putty roll
- Rags
- Simple Green (see Product Sources)
- 220- or 320-grit abrasive paper
- Firm sanding block

Step 1: Choose a shade of epoxy putty roll that is close to, or slightly lighter than, the surface being repaired. Cut off a piece of the putty and knead the two parts together until the color is uniform (see **Figure 7.9**).

Step 2: Apply the putty into the damage, pressing firmly. Remove the excess and smooth it out with a rag dampened with full-strength Simple Green (see **Figure 7.10**). Be careful not to soak the area because this product is strong and can remove some finishes.

Step 3: When the epoxy has cured, sand it flush; then color and over-finish as described on page 171.

Figure 7.9. Knead a suitable slice of the putty roll until the color is uniform.

Helpful Tip ———

Texturizing Wood

For grainy woods, you must "texturize" a patch to mimic the surrounding area. Use a single-edge razor blade to scratch grain lines into applied burn-in stick and epoxy putty while it is still semi-soft (see **Figure 7.11**).

Figure 7.11. Even a perfect color match will be noticeable if the texture doesn't match. Carefully, scratch "grain" into the filler while it is still semi-soft.

Figure 7.10. A Simple Green dampened rag will smooth and remove excess putty.

Replacing Color and Over-Finishing

Sometimes older finishes are worn through, exposing bare wood. In the simplest cases, that will require new finish (over-finishing). In most cases, it will first require coloring the wood to match the original coloring. Use a small amount of color, and do not build thick piles of the mix because it will look murky. Start lighter in color and sneak up on the match with a slightly darker mix.

Step 1: Clean the area thoroughly.

Step 2: Place a glass piece on the surface. Dip a brush into the shellac first and then right into the dry powders. Mix the shellac and powder on the piece of glass, and compare your color to the color of the surface (see **Figure 7.12**). Tweak the color with the powders until it matches.

Step 3: Layer very thin coats of your color mix onto the worn spots. Keep the mix wet with the shellac and work thinly and quickly (see **Figure 7.13**).

Step 4: If the color match doesn't satisfy you after it dries, you may be able to tweak it with an appropriate glaze, lightly applied and wiped off. Allow the glaze to dry; then seal it gently with shellac, or spray a light coat from an aerosol.

Step 5: If the repair area is small, you can over-finish with aerosols (see **Figure 7.14**). Choose the closest sheen available. To over-finish the entire surface, use a wipe-on product like Wipe-On Poly. If color is missing, then a good choice is one of the colored oils, such as Watco, to blend troublesome areas (see **Figure 7.15**). Apply as many coats as necessary to make the piece look good.

Tools and Materials
- Dry powder colors (from Behlen or Homestead)
- Shellac
- Artist brushes
- 1" x 3" or 4" clear glass scraps
- Glaze in an appropriate color
- Shellac or aerosol topcoat
- Wipe-on polyurethane or colored finishing oil

Figure 7.12. Blending colors on a small piece of glass makes it easy to compare the mix with the existing finish.

Figure 7.13. An artist's brush and a steady hand produce a neat application.

Figure 7.14. Aerosol topcoats are ideal for small areas that must blend with the surrounding area.

Figure 7.15. Oils are particularly convenient for replacing color on convoluted surfaces.

Repolishing a Worn Finish

Since "wear" typically consists of a multitude of very shallow scratches, polishing with very fine abrasives eliminates them by removing a very thin amount of topcoat. If you do it too often, you'll cut right through to the wood, of course, but a multi-layer topcoat in good condition can often be restored to like-new condition with no more than repolishing.

Tools and Materials

- 1000-, 1500-, and 2000-grit wet/dry abrasive paper
- Oil and mineral spirit lubricant
- Firm sanding block
- Swirl remover or paste wax
- Rags

Step 1: Repolishing is much like rubbing out as explained in Full Rub-Out for Brush-On Finishes, page 124. Begin with leveling. Use a 1000 or 1500 grit with the oil and mineral spirit lubricant (see **Figure 7.16**). Work carefully and check that you aren't cutting through the finish. The scratches should smooth away with the fine abrasive. Continue into 1500 and then 2000 grit. If you cut through the finish and color in places, go to Replacing Color and Over-Finishing, on page 171.

Step 2: Finish with a swirl remover or paste wax (see **Figure 7.17**).

Figure 7.16. Polish out the scratches but no more; check often.

Figure 7.17. A swirl remover, sold primarily to the auto refinishing trade, will remove the very finest scratches left by the 2000-grit abrasive.

Adventures in Finishing

Now that I have equipped you with techniques to deal with most damage, let me tell you a story of a table with damage I couldn't deal with.

The estimate was for an older couple, probably Italian, from the old country. The husband sat quietly in the other room while the wife talked with me. We were talking about their maple table that they had bought when first married. It had survived all of their children and all of their dramas and now needed refinishing badly. I gave her a price, and she checked with the Mister. Given the green light, the job was mine. I completed it in the allotted time and delivered it. Everyone was happy. But not the end of the story!

A few months later, I received a call from this couple. It seems where the mister sat every day for his dinner, the finish was doing something bad. I went over and looked at it. Yes, it was wearing, but it was a mystery to me how it could happen so quickly. I took it back to the shop and cleaned it, over-finished it, and repolished it. Delivered and done. But not the end of the story!

Another few months and another call. The same table with the same problem. I couldn't figure out what the problem was. This man was causing the problem at the exact location where his arms rested on the table. What in the world was she feeding him? Hydrochloric acid? Was the Italian diet that corrosive? I took the table back and refinished that half of the table. I polished it out and returned it. This time I gave her a source to buy table pads. The mister was just too much for the finish!

Care of furniture: myths and malarkey!

Genuine antiques, legitimate historical artifacts, are precious and deserve special care. Family heirlooms, even when they are not antiques, are also precious within the family and may deserve equal care. When I discuss antiques and heirlooms with clients, or restore the finish on such an item, I always advise them on proper care. And I always give a client a page of information on care and continued maintenance of the new or restored finish.

Popular "wisdom" on the proper care for furniture finishes is full of myths, malarkey, and advertising nonsense. To sort out the valuable information we have to ask why we finish wood to begin with. There are three reasons:

1. To make the wood beautiful.
2. To protect the wood from grime, grease, and everyday messes.
3. To minimize the expansion and contraction of the wood by providing a barrier against moisture from the environment.

Figure 7.18. The boards have shrunk across the grain; the end-cap has not shrunk with the grain. The only practical prevention of the problem is an environment humid enough to maintain the original moisture content of the wood.

Common Myths

With these three reasons in mind, the goal is to maintain the finish so it can keep doing its job of beautification, protection, and minimization of movement. But first consider that maintenance methods are only necessary when there is a threat, such as exposure to moisture or scuffing. In some cases, the better solution may be climate control, better housekeeping, or totally different materials for highly abusive situations. Let's examine some of the common myths surrounding wood finishes and the care and "feeding" of them.

Myth #1: A finish can prevent shrinking and expanding

Woodworkers are well aware that wood shrinks when it dries and expands when it absorbs moisture, but unfortunately no practical finish can prevent this shrinking and expanding. A well-chosen and maintained finish can, however, slow it down enough that shrinkage during the dry time of the year followed by expansion during the humid time of the year is small enough that no structural damage is done. But, if you take a piece of furniture from an area with a high annual average humidity such as Florida to an area with a low annual average humidity such as Arizona, then, over a short time, the wood will dry out and shrink. It may well crack and fall apart regardless of the finish or its condition. The only practical way to prevent damage in such a case is to provide an artificially high humidity (see **Figure 7.18**).

Myth #2: Climate control is just for humans

Most of us think of climate control in terms of personal comfort. Museums think of it as essential protection for their valuable collections. It serves both objectives. The rule of thumb is "If you are comfortable, then your furniture is too." Humidification, dehumidification, and temperature control can all help make both you and your furniture more comfortable and longer lasting.

Myth #3: If the wood has a durable finish, it can withstand almost any treatment

The finishes that can do a reasonable job of protecting furniture from dirt and annual wood movement include urethanes, varnishes, lacquers, and shellac—provided they are well maintained. Timely housekeeping can prevent a lot of irreversible damage, but it's not always practical in today's hectic world. If a household has three kids, two cats, and a dog and everyone rushes out to school and work in the morning, then the spilled milk and Fruit Loops sit on the table all day. When the cat knocks over the vase full of water on it, no one is there to pick it up until six o'clock that night. There are households that would be best furnished with an industrial stainless steel table in the kitchen. Fine finishes on fine furniture are not always appropriate for everyday use in today's hectic households (see **Figure 7.19**).

Myth #4: Some finishes are bulletproof

Which finishes offer little or no protection at all, and which ones are bulletproof? If the table with the Fruit Loops had a wax or "butcher block" finish (basically mineral oil), then Mom and Dad have a problem. Neither one of these finishes provides protection for the wood.

If the table had Danish oil on it, there is a chance that the oil, though damaged, could be repaired. After 10 to 12 hours, however, the water and milk will probably migrate into the wood and stain it. Then, the finish will have to be removed, the stains removed, and a new finish applied. Danish oil is not a good choice for kids and pets. An appropriate finish for the Fruit Loops gang is in the "bulletproof" category. Strictly speaking, there is no such thing. No practical finish is capable of tolerating all types of abuse including standing water or milk, and heat. All finishes will eventually break down.

However, if the table had a multi-coat film finish in good condition, it had a chance of surviving until someone came home to clean up. A factory finish such as a pre-catalyzed lacquer is a good choice for a family with kids. The maintenance on a finish like this is easy to live with; simply wipe up after meals with a damp cloth. Twice a year clean it thoroughly with a mild furniture detergent (Murphy Oil Soap or Behlen's Wool Lube) and then paste wax. That's it! No feeding, no oiling; those are myths!

Figure 7.19. Spilt milk and fine furniture are not the best of partners.

Figure 7.20. That's not a shadow under the jug; it's the original color of the table.

Myth #5: Cleaning the furniture every day keeps it free from danger

The elderly spinster who spends half of every day cleaning house may not need a "bulletproof" topcoat, but her furniture is not free of all danger. Lift the vase from the center of the table in front of her dining room window and notice the circle of color. It's the color of the table in its former life. No wood finishing product is impervious to degradation from light. Sunlight is powerful; it both darkens and bleaches wood and fades stains. Protected areas soon contrast with the unprotected areas around them (see **Figure 7.20**). Educating yourself or your client and then using drapes or tablecloths is the only practical way to protect a furniture finish from the sun.

Myth #6: Wood must be fed

A lot of people fall prey to furniture polish hype. The marketers will tell you that the wood has to be fed! It must be oiled before it dies and shrivels up! They make it sound like wood is a living, breathing creature. But wood is not alive. Furthermore, a protective finish on furniture will prevent oil in a maintenance product from reaching the wood just as effectively as it will prevent unwanted spills from reaching the wood. Furniture polishes park on top of the finish where they may even attract dust. The hype is as superficial as the product.

Myth #7: Finishes can always be rejuvenated

Rejuvenating a finish that has lived its life span and has now started to deteriorate is a myth; there is no fountain of youth for wood finishes. If a film finish has fractures, crazing, or worn or missing areas, you cannot re-polish or oil it back to youthful perfection. The piece needs a new finish.

Some products claim to "re-amalgamate" a finish. These products sometimes work on reversible finishes (shellac and regular lacquer) if they are not too damaged (see **Figure 7.21**). The solvents in these "restorer products" soften the finish and "re-flow" it back to a consistent film. At best, they can delay refinishing. At their worst, they create a sticky mess that is more work than refinishing.

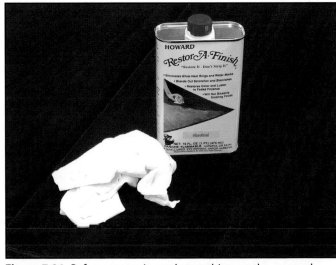

Figure 7.21. Before you try it, read everything on the can and make sure you understand *all* of it.

The Truth and Malarkey of Furniture Care Products

The number of furniture care products on the market is overwhelming. (The usefulness of many of them is underwhelming.) There are polishes in bottles and spray cans; there are spray waxes and paste waxes galore; there are colored oils and oils with citrus scents in them. How do you decide what to use? It would be handy if they could be divided up into neat categories, but with a few exceptions that's not the case.

Truth: Paste waxes are worth using

Paste waxes are worth using because they are comparatively inexpensive, provide limited but real benefits, and do no harm. The price of a one-pound can of high-quality paste wax may not seem inexpensive, but, in the typical household it will last practically forever, long after you've used dozens of cans of highly advertised spray products.

The best quality paste waxes are blends of carnauba or candelilla, beeswax, and sometimes paraffin. Too much paraffin in a blend will make it too soft and smudgy. Too much of the harder waxes will make it too difficult to buff out. Bowling alley wax, for example, is a hard floor wax intended for polishing out with a floor buffer. It's totally unsuitable for furniture! Pure beeswax, on the other hand, is way too soft; it is most useful in a blend with hard waxes to make them manageable. I've found that Behlen's Blue Label Wax (also known as Staples Premium Paste Wax) is an excellent blend and that Liberon's paste waxes are quite good (see **Figure 7.22**).

Helpful Tip —————————————

When to Wax a New Finish

All waxes are made with solvents to keep them smooth and easy to use. Most have toluene and other solvents in them. Some more recent formulations are toluene free. These solvents are all too strong for newly finished wood. Never, ever, wax a brand-new film finish with paste wax. It will soften the finish. Wait for the finish to cure for at least a week or two, preferably a month.

The big benefit of paste wax is in the surface properties that it imparts to your furniture. A waxed surface is somewhat slippery without being greasy, and liquids tend to bead up rather than spread out or soak in. Stuff that might tend to scuff a less slippery surface can't seem to get a grip on a waxed surface. The dry, non-greasy surface doesn't "grab" dust and other particles, so they are easier to clean up. Spilled liquids don't "wet" the surface, making it easier to clean them up as well.

Perhaps most importantly, paste waxes do no harm. They go where you put them without spills or overspray, and, once the solvents in them have evaporated, they are quite innocuous. (See the Helpful Tip box on page 176 for a precaution on when to apply them.) If your furniture is damaged, you'll be glad that the only product on the surface is paste wax, which can be easily removed with mineral spirits, and not unknowns or silicone, which is difficult to remove thoroughly and interferes with refinishing. If you value your furniture, follow the example of museums; they won't put anything but the highest quality non-acid paste wax on antiques that are worth millions.

When applying a paste wax, start with a surface that can be buffed out easily before going on to the next surface. Don't apply wax on the entire piece before buffing. Apply a thin layer, and then buff with a clean cloth. This is not an automobile wax; it doesn't need to haze up hard before polishing out (see **Figure 7.23**).

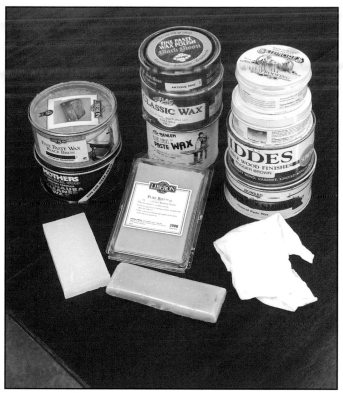

Figure 7.22. There's no shortage of choices in waxes. My personal preference is Behlen's Blue Label.

Figure 7.23. For more control over the amount of wax being applied, scoop out a lump of wax, fold it up in a square of cloth, and press or squeeze the wax out of the pad as you apply it.

Helpful Tip _____

Color-Matching Waxes

Uncolored wax can fill open grain or deeply carved parts of your furniture and turn white when it dries. A matching-color wax is invisible after it's dry (see **Figure 7.24**).

Figure 7.24. Match the wax to the color of the furniture to avoid white wax buildup in grain pores or carved crevices.

Truth: Choose your cleaning aids wisely

Cleaning aids are all over store shelves and TV screens for good reasons; housecleaning is an out-of-favor chore, and the family member primarily responsible for it is also frequently the one who does the shopping. My advice is not to dispense with them but to choose wisely.

Advisable furniture cleaning, other than cleaning up messes, falls into two categories: routine dusting and periodic thorough cleaning. Until fairly recently there were few practical choices for routine dusting: a dry dust cloth that tended to move dust around as much as it picked it up, a treated dust cloth that tended to leave a residue (in some cases adhesive) on the surface, and a slightly damp dust cloth. Of the three, the damp cloth was clearly the best. Now, however, technology has come up with a fourth contender with genuine merit. It is a 70% polyester, 30% polyamide, lint-free, washable, and non-abrasive microcloth (see **Figure 7.25**). It doesn't need the wet pick-up provided by water, polishes, or oils. The fibers in these cloths are 200 times finer than the hair on your head and do an excellent job of picking up dust.

Periodic thorough cleaning is a chore but a necessary one if you want to take good care of your furniture, whether manufactured, hand crafted, or heirloom. The foremost rule is the same here as it is in medical practice: "Do no harm." Before running to the store to get the latest high-tech product on the advice of the marketing department of the manufacturer, learn what the ingredients are, why they are in the product, and what their short- and long-term effects may be on your valuable furniture. I don't have time for that. That's why I stick with a simple, low-tech, proven-over-time, biodegradable, phosphate-free product: Murphy Oil Soap. It takes less time and effort to just do it than to make sure the latest alternative is safe. Mix ⅛ to ¼ cup in a half-gallon of water and wipe your furniture with a wrung-out cloth. Allow any dampness to evaporate, and then apply paste wax as described above.

Malarkey: Furniture oils have many benefits for furniture

Furniture oils are widely touted by their many makers for furniture care. Some have orange or lemon scents in them. Some are colored to disguise scratches. Because they have

Figure 7.25. Originally used in "clean room" environments, microcloths are excellent for dusting. They hold static electricity to pick up more dust.

mineral oil and/or mineral spirits in them, they leave a very temporary oil slick on the surface. They may smell nice, or make you feel better, but they don't do a thing for the wood or the furniture. Antique dealers use gallons of it for a temporary "glow" at the sales counter (see **Figure 7.26**).

Truth: Other waxes, polishes, and cleaners have some advantages and disadvantages

The grand collection of remaining waxes, polishes, and cleaners have various oil and petroleum products in them— some have emulsified oil and water, some have silicone for slickness, and some are water based. You'll find them in bottles and spray cans. The wet ones help pick up dust and provide a temporary shiny surface. Silicone isn't a bad ingredient, but refinishers curse it because it interferes with adhesion of the new finish. Just keep in mind that the advertisers will claim benefits for their products but won't tell you the disadvantages, and even your friends are more likely to tell you their good experiences than their disappointments.

Figure 7.26. Furniture oils are not care or maintenance products at all. They give a superficial glow and pleasant scent, that's all.

Some Final Thoughts on Furniture Care

By now you may be looking around at all the furniture that you have been "feeding" with oil, or you may have built a piece on commission and want to give the client good advice on how to care for it, or your neighbor in Arizona may have just brought home a nice antique New England chest and wants to know how to care for it. Just what kind of care does furniture need?

For the well-fed wood, just stop the oiling. If you can't keep yourself from oiling, be aware that you are just providing a temporary shiny surface and profits for the manufacturers.

If the commission piece has a new film finish on it, wait a few weeks or more and then wax it with paste wax. If you finished it with Danish oil, go ahead and apply its first coat of paste wax. Explain to your client how to apply wax and hand over a new can of it. Providing a page of care information is also a nice touch and emphasizes the importance of proper care. On the sheet, mention that the finish cannot withstand heat, standing water, or strong sunlight, and stress the importance of hot mats, coasters, and curtains for shade.

If your neighbor with the antique New England chest doesn't already know, explain that the room it is going in must be climate controlled to provide a New England environment, just like a museum would provide. The wax must be micro crystalline (man-made) to avoid acids, such as Renaissance Wax. If controlling the climate isn't possible, take it back to New England where it was comfortable for 300 years.

Between the once or twice a year paste waxing, dust with one of the new microcloths. And what do you do about the all-day milk and Fruit Loops? Consider *Form*ica—for the *form*ative years!

Helpful Tip ———————————

Wax Buildup

Wax does not build up on a surface if it's buffed out. Each application dissolves the old layer and any excess is buffed out. If it is not buffed out, then yes, it will build up.

Restoration and conservation

When talking about giving special care to your fine furniture, antiques, and family heirlooms, the question of restoration often comes up. For me, antiques and fine furniture have been a lifelong passion. At the very young age of 14, I had a summer job of painting houses, including one that belonged to a fine arts dealer. After the house was painted, I stayed on to work part-time. One of my tasks involved a period antique Queen Anne rosewood chair that had suffered greatly from smoke and soot but was not scorched. The dealer set me out by the barn with a bucket of denatured alcohol and showed me how to wash down the chair the old-fashioned way. As the alcohol and black soot drizzled down the back of the chair and revealed gleaming rosewood underneath, my life literally turned on a dime. The passion of finding a jewel in the rough and resurrecting it to its former glory set me on fire! This, I knew, was my lifetime pursuit!

Little did I know it was to be a lifetime education of studying the history of furniture up close and hands-on. Every piece I came across had a story to tell from the wear and damage it had suffered along the way. These pieces also told me when they were made as I disassembled and re-glued them. Some of the clues were the finely cut dovetails in an early piece with slight irregularities from hand cutting. The machine dovetails revealed the later factory furniture from the turn of the last century (see **Figure 7.27**). The type of wood, finishes, and hardware were also indications of when the piece was made. All of this information was collected and summarized in my mental file to allow me to make the correct decision on what to do next and how to proceed in the resurrection process. The market was very clear on values—if it was "early" or "of the period," as antique dealers put it, leave it alone. It brought more money when it had its original surface.

Figure 7.27. Hand-cut dovetails (on the top drawer) or machine-cut dovetails (on the bottom drawer) help define the age of a piece.

A Short History of the Antiques Market

I was fortunate to live in New Hampshire at a time when beautiful antiques were pouring forth from barns and attics with seemingly no end to the supply. There were estate auctions, tag sales, and barn sales anywhere from the backwoods to cow pastures all over New England. The largest source—the Sunday flea market in southern New Hampshire—had an enormous selection of early painted plank seat chairs, blanket chests, Windsor chairs, pie safes, and tall case clocks from the late seventeen and early eighteen hundreds (see **Figure 7.28** to **Figure 7.30**). Later furniture included rolltop desks, hall trees, Hoosier cabinets, and marble top bedroom sets from the 1880s with the high-back beds and curved footboards the size of battle-ships (see **Figure 7.31**). It was an exciting and fortuitous time to be in the antique business. It also augmented my education rapidly when I would see a highboy fresh from the barn, filthy and partially rotten on the feet, sell on the field for thousands. It was eye-opening to watch the early (early as in 5 a.m. and as in period antiques) buyers running to get these pieces and pulling a wad of hundred dollar bills out of their pocket to pay gladly for these barn rats!

Figure 7.28. A beautiful primitive cupboard, a Boston rocker, a one-drawer stand, and a Sheraton grain painted chair.

Figure 7.29. A plethora of great antiques used to pour out of barns; not any longer.

Regrettably, those days are forever gone. The barns and attics have some antiques left, but the number of dealers, auction houses, and "e-bayers" have created a gritty competitive market that has taken the fun out of it. One of the largest contributors to the change in the market is the *Antiques Roadshow.* The average person who might have attic jewels has seen the appraisals of pieces on this show that look just like what they have, and the Keno Brothers have said it is worth fifty thousand! Or it was mentioned on the show that a piece was refinished and was worth fifty thousand before it was stripped but now is only worth ten. Wow! With these snapshots of information, everyone is "afraid" of their antiques. The barn-filthy oak Victorian chest sits in a house untouched because it is an antique (see **Figure 7.32**). Truly, this piece needs a total overhaul, but the owner thinks it will be stripped of its value. This is an example of not enough information to make a wise decision on what to do next.

It is more than 37 years later from that day of the sooty rosewood chair. The wild antiquing frontier in New England is gone, but the restoration business is very good. Part of this business is an educational process in which I can share my experience from those frontier days of seeing and handling so much furniture. When I quote a homeowner on a restoration job, invariably the *Antiques Roadshow* comes up in the conversation. The value of the piece and the question of whether or not to restore it (because of the TV show) lead to the discussion and inspection of the piece. The drawers are pulled out to examine the construction detail, the hardware, and the internal part of the piece. The timeline of when it was inherited or how long it has been in the family is also discussed. This is the very first step in the discovery process of deciding if the item should be restored or conserved. This is called an appraisal. Once you do your homework, the answer will be obvious.

Courtesy Heritage Center of Lancaster County

Figure 7.30.
A gorgeous tall case clock from Lancaster, Pennsylvania, crafted by an unknown cabinetmaker circa 1790.

Figure 7.31. A walnut relic from the days when beds were 8'- to 10'-tall battleships.

Figure 7.32. This is a true "barn rat," needing all the help it can get.

Appraisals: Self Generated, *Antiques Roadshow* Generated, Professionally Generated

The worst appraisals often come from family "lore" that has been passed down from one generation to another. I remember once instance that happened when I went to see a Singer sewing machine. The owner swore it was 300 years old! (That was what he was told.) Simply reading the patent date of 1915 on the bobbin plate would have gone a long way in dispelling that information! So, how does a non-antique person find out just what it is that they have? There are several methods.

Self-generated appraisals: Libraries are a good source of information, but it is difficult to have a conversation with a book (see **Figure 7.33**). Local antique dealers are sometimes helpful, but they are in business to buy. They can at least tell you what they might pay for it and possibly how old it is, or even have something similar on the showroom floor. The Internet and e-bay can be a helpful source, but the information can be a little sketchy. These are all forms of self-generated appraisals.

***Antiques Roadshow*-generated appraisals:** The Antiques Roadshow is a source of information, but the likelihood of a piece coming up that is identical to the one in your house is remote. And you can't actually touch the piece that is on TV.

Professionally generated appraisals: The professional appraiser is often the most efficient way of getting the most accurate information. Choose a qualified appraiser that actually specializes in furniture. A jewelry appraiser could potentially be just as in the dark as you are about furniture. The cost for a non-insurance appraisal could be just a flat fee—ask first.

Figure 7.33. Books can be a great starting point for gathering information about your furniture, but a professional appraiser is a better choice if you have specific questions about your pieces.

Appraisal Done, Now What?

The appraiser came and provided the information about the piece. It goes something like this: A fine example of early 1800s Federal chest in the style of Pennsylvania cabinetmaking (see **Figure 7.34**). The condition is very fine, with original surface and hardware. The feet are full length, but the drawer runners are slightly worn. Or they said this: The chest is an oak five-drawer chest with the Larkin Soap Co. label on the back. Manufactured about 1910, missing some of its hardware, and the finish is badly deteriorated.

Good! Congratulations. You are now armed with almost too much information. Well, no, you have exactly the right information. Significant to the first piece is the date and that it was handmade by cabinetmakers in a particular geographic area. This is called provenance—a proven historical point and location in time. The condition is almost pristine and the surface has never been refinished. What do you do with this piece? Raise your insurance. Conserve with conservator's wax once a year. Other than that, do nothing.

The second piece immediately tells you about itself with the word "manufactured." It is part of a plentiful group of furniture that was turned out from factories at the turn of the last century by the boatload. It has no significant historical connection to an individual cabinetmaker. It does have a label, which is nice. It gives a little history as to what company it came from. What do you do with this piece? Everything. Restore it by stripping and refinishing it, replace the hardware, and enjoy it as a vintage piece of good, serviceable furniture (see **Figure 7.35**).

Figure 7.34. An early Federal cherry chest of drawers from Pennsylvania—"right as rain."

Figure 7.35. Here's a chest similar to the "barn rat" from Figure 7.32. After a total overhaul, it's restored to its former glory and is back in service.

CHAPTER 7 – REPAIR AND RESTORATION

Figure 7.36. Is it Gustav Stickley or isn't it?

Figure 7.37. An incredible Deco-style writing desk in Macassar ebony and pearwood, made by Kent Townsend in the style of Jacques Emil Ruhlmann.

Rule of thumb: If the piece is pre-1850, be very cautious. Stay firmly planted in the conservation laws. The definition of conservation is to stabilize and conserve the piece as it exists right now. All efforts must be reversible. If the piece is post-1850, the rules relax a bit. For most pieces, if the condition is undesirable or deplorable, restore it. The definition of restoration is to bring the piece back to "as new condition" as closely as possible. This would still include rules of staying with the appropriate finish, hardware, etc.

However—wouldn't it be good if life were simple and clear-cut—even in this restorable group there are subgroups that could potentially be compromised in value if restored. These could include pieces made or designed by Carlo Bugatti, Belter, Gustav Stickley, Greene and Greene, Wallace Nutting, George Nakashima, and high-end Art Nouveau and Art Deco such as Emil Galle and Jacques Emil Ruhlmann, and many more (see **Figure 7.36** to **Figure 7.37**). The market demands that these examples be "straight and right" to get the price tags that resemble telephone

Figure 7.38. A Queen Anne writing table in tiger maple with "Dutch" feet, made and finished by the author.

Figure 7.39. A Federal two-drawer inlaid tiger maple stand, made and finished by the author.

numbers. These pieces land in the post-1850 "restore it" group (some of them are even into the 1930s and 1940s) but need to adhere to the pre-1850s conservation rules because of their desirability, exclusivity, and rarity.

Also out there in the big world of antiques are the "foolers." Pictured are several pieces that look like period antiques in the pre-1850 group but are not (see **Figure 7.38** to **Figure 7.41**). These are contemporary reproduc-

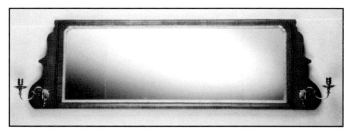

Figure 7.40. A Queen Anne chimney mirror in tiger maple, complete with a gilded and incised gesso liner around the mirror. Crafted by the author.

Figure 7.41. A Federal tapered leg stand in tiger maple with banded drawers and shaped skirts. Crafted by the author.

tions that can be lumped into the post-1850 "go ahead and restore if needed" group. These are the "new" antiques that may someday be worth something.

Appraising the Owner of the Piece

Finally, the actual owner of the piece is the last part of the equation. If the person is the end owner and will never sell it, the final decision rests in their heart. They can ultimately choose to live with it in any condition they want, including making it brand spanking new!

If the owner is a collector who has invested in the piece, they may choose only to stabilize it to conserve their investment as well as the piece. If the owner is an antique dealer, their decision will be based on financial gain. The most value will be in the optimum condition to acquire that value. Years ago, an old Yankee told me, "You make your money when you buy it." If a dealer has purchased an early, period, all original, antique slant-front desk that sits in the shop waiting for the right buyer (see **Figure 7.42**), it is already making money. This dealer knows not to touch it.

Or like a wise dealer from Vermont once told me (kind of a "beauty is in the eye" thing), "I buy junk and sell antiques!" He was a very wealthy man!

Figure 7.42. An outstanding example of a slant-front desk in tiger maple from New London, Connecticut, circa 1760.

Product Description	Home Centers	Homestead (mail order)	Woodcraft (mail & stores)	Woodworker's Supply (mail & stores)	Klingspor (mail & stores)	Sherwin Williams (stores)	Highland Hardware (mail & stores)	Touch Up Depot (mail order)	Local stores
2-part epoxy			x	x	x			x	marine
3M Scotchbrite in rolls						x			auto body supply
3M Stikit paper in rolls			x	x				x	auto body supply
Aniline dyes		x	x	x	x		x		
Artist brushes	x	x	x	x	x	x	x	x	art supply
Badger brushes		x	x	x	x				
Bartley's Clear Gel Varnish		x	x	x					
Bartley's gel stains		x	x	x				x	
Behlen's 15-Minute Wood Stain				x					
Behlen's Master Colors		x		x					
Behlen's Master Gel				x	x				
Behlen's Pore-O-Pac grain filler		x	x	x	x			PB	
Behlen's Shading and Glazing stain		x	x	x	x				
Behlen's Solar-Lux dye stains		x	x	x	x			x	auto body supply
Behlen's Solar-Lux retarder		x	x	x			x		
Behlen's wood stain reducer				x					
Behlen's Wool Lube		x	x	x	x	x		PB	auto body supply
Bloxygen		x	x	x	x		x		
Bondo	x					x			auto body supply
Bullseye Sealcoat			x	x	x			x	paint
Burlap				x					fabric
Burn-in knife and sticks		x	x	x	x		x	x	
CA (super) glue	x	x	x	x	x		x	x	paint
Chip brushes	x			x		x	x	x	paint
Chroma-Chem 844 colorants								x	paint
Clearwater Color stains				x			x		
Cupran, Reduran hand cleaners		x						x	
Danish oils	x		x	x	x	x	x		paint
Deft brushing lacquer	x								paint
Dry pigment powders		x	x	x	x			x	
Epoxy colorants			x				x		
Epoxy dough stick			x	x	x			x	
Fill sticks		x	x	x	x	x		x	
General oil- and water-based stains			x	x	x				
General polyacrylic finish			x	x	x	x	x		
General Seal A Cell			x	x	x				auto body supply
Gloves	x			x	x	x	x	x	hardware
Goof Off	x								grocery
Japan colors		x		x				x	art supply
Lacquer aerosols	x	x	x	x	x	x	x	x	paint
Masters Brush Cleaner				x					art supply
Mica powders				x					art supply
Minwax stains	x					x			paint
Mirka Abralon discs		x		x					

	1	2	3	4	5	6	7	8	Source
Mirka Royal micro discs		x		x					
Mohawk products, retail									OFS, Inc.
Oily rag can				x			x		Grainger
Paint filters	x			x		x		x	paint
Paraffin, mineral oil		x	x	x	x				grocery
Paste waxes	x	x	x	x	x	x	x	x	X
Plastic scrapers	x			x					paint
Pumice, rottenstone		x		x	x	x			
Respirator	x			x	x	x	x	x	auto body supply
Sanding block, cork		x		x			x	x	
Sanding block, felt		x	x	x	x		x		
Sanding discs	x	x	x	x	x		x	x	hardware
Sandpaper, sheets	x	x	x	x	x	x	x	x	hardware
Sherwin Williams glazes									company store
Sherwin Williams grain filler									company store
Sherwin Williams wiping stains						x			company store
Silicon carbide wet-or-dry paper		x	x	x	x	x	x		paint
Simple Success water base				x					
Solvents	x		x	x	x	x	x		paint
Steel wool, 0000	pads		rolls	both	pads	pads	pads	both	paint
Tack cloths	x			x	x	x	x	x	paint
Taklon water base and shellac brush		x		x					
TintsAll colorant and UTC's	x			x		x	x	x	paint
Trans Star Tri Cut or 3M Perfect It		x		x					auto body supply
TransTint or Wizard Tints		x	x	x			x	x	
Tung oil			x	x	x		x	x	
Un-Du Adhesive Remover				x					
Varathane stains					x		x		paint
Watco oil in colors and clear	x		x	x	x	x	x		paint
Watco Wipe-On Poly	x		x	x	x	x	x		paint
Waterlox products		x	x	x			x		direct
Wood Prep, Franklin glue size				x					paint
Wood putty	x	x	x	x	x	x	x	x	paint
Woodburst stains			x	x					

PB: Private Brand

Manufacturers' and Suppliers' Phone Numbers and Web Addresses

Behlen products	www.hbehlen.com	(800) 545-0047	Mohawk retail outlet: OFS, Inc.		(800) 381-3126
Highland Hardware	www.highlandhardware.com	(800) 241-6748	Old-Fashioned Milk Paint Co., Groton, MA.		(978) 448-6336
Homestead Finishing Products	www.homesteadfinishing.com	(216) 631-5309	The Real Milk Paint Co.	www.realmilkpaint.com	(800) 339-9748
Klingspor	www.woodworkingshop.com	(800) 228-0000	Rockler Hardware	www.rockler.com	(800) 279-4441
Lee Valley Tools Ltd.	www.leevalley.com	(800) 267-8735	Sherwin Williams	www.sherwin-williams.com	(800) 474-3794
3M Corporation	www.3M.com	(888) 364-3577	Touch-Up Depot	www.touchupdepot.com	(866) 883-3768
Merit Industries	www.meritindustries.com		Waterlox	www.waterlox.com	(216) 641-4877
Mirka Abrasives	www.mirka-usa.com	(800) 843-3904	Woodcraft	www.woodcraft.com	(800) 225-1153
Mohawk	www.mohawk-finishing.com	(800) 545-0047	Woodworker's Supply	www.woodworker.com	(800) 645-9292

GLOSSARY

Binder: An additive that mixes with a pigment to allow the particles of color to "stick" to the wood piece.

Bleeding: The occurrence of open-grained woods popping oil from their pores when they are finished with oils. The oils pop out of the pores while drying, and if not wiped away, bleeding will cause dried dots of oil on the surface.

Blotching: Uneven coloration that occurs when wood absorbs stain unevenly.

Chip brush: A cheap brush made of China bristle that is perfect for finishing.

Colored Danish oil: A pigmented oil with a higher proportion of oil than pigment that builds a light film on the surface of wood without obscuring the grain. Danish oil, whether colored or clear, provides only minimal protection.

Conditioning: Lightly sealing wood before finishing to limit absorption of stain and prevent blotching.

Dewhiskering: The process of dampening wood with water and sanding down raised grain before finishing with a water-based stain.

Distressing: Intentionally adding wear on a finished surface to achieve an antique look, especially in combination with milk paint.

Dye: A type of wood colorant that gives a transparent, evenly penetrated finish. Fades more quickly than pigment.

Fill sticks: Hole filler, available in a variety of colors. Cleaner than putty—topcoats and sealers can be applied right over.

Gel stain: An ideal stain for woods that tend to accept stain unevenly, as the gel consistency of the product limits its absorption. Also useful for applying stain to surfaces that cannot be laid flat; the consistency of the product prevents it from running down in streaks.

Glaze: A product that adds a subtle dimension of color, highlights, or creates an antique look. Glazes are almost always used on sealed surfaces.

Gloss finish: A shiny, polished-looking finish.

Glue size: A water-based sizing that is mixed with warm water and used to condition wood. Glue size also facilitates the easy removal of "fuzzies" on the wood by hardening them so they are easily sanded off.

Grain filling: Filling the tiny natural voids in open-grained woods with a silica-based material.

Japan colors: A heavy bodied concentrated pigment suspended in a varnish-like medium that can be used as a tint or diluted to make a stain.

Highly figured wood: Wood with a vibrantly detailed and unique grain pattern, such as tiger or bird's-eye maple.

Lacquer: A fast drying brush-on topcoat that provides decent protection.

Lap marks: "Stop-and-start" marks that can occur when using a water-soluble aniline dye. Lap marks are easily removed by immediately rubbing with a water-dampened rag.

Leveling: Wet sanding with a mineral oil/mineral spirit lubricant to clean up puddles or ridges left after a finish dries.

Lorient brush: A natural bristle brush made of hog bristles that is used to apply oil-based topcoats and brushing lacquer.

Material Safety Data Sheets (MSDS): A useful reference that outlines the hazards of products.

Milk paint: A delicate finish highly prized for antique reproduction. Used by the early American settlers and on Shaker antiques.

Non-grain-raising (NGR) stain: Dye stain that dissolves in alcohol and does not raise the grain, as water-based dyes do. NGR stains dry quickly and are best applied with a spray gun, unless a retarder is used.

Oil-based urethane: An oil based urethane/polyurethane that is usually brushed out and gives a warm color to wood. This finish can yellow light woods and yellows over time.

Padding on: A technique used to apply shellac as a topcoat.

Penetrating oil: See colored Danish oil.

Piano finish: A glasslike surface.

Pigment: A type of wood colorant that requires a binder and creates an opaque, fade-resistant color finish.

Polyurethane: Another term to describe a urethane finish. Poly, meaning more than one, refers to the resin or resins that make up this finish. A durable finish suitable for high use objects. Difficult to touch up if damaged.

Prefinishing: Finishing the pieces of a project before assembly in order to avoid finish inconsistencies resulting from wood movement.

Pumice: Finely-ground lava, used for polishing, that breaks down as it is used.

Rottenstone: Powdered limestone used for polishing.

Rubbing out: Various methods used to smooth or polish out a finish after it is cured. Using 0000 steel wool and wax to remove subtle inconsistencies and blemishes from finishing is an example of rubbing out. Also known as finishing the finish.

Sap streaks: White streaks in wood caused by a vein of sap. Depending on the desired effect of the piece, sap streaks may have to be cut out or colored in.

Satin finish: A low luster sheen of finish.

Shellac: A delicate, easy to apply finish. Ideal for sealing tabletop bottoms and the interiors of drawers and chests.

Solvent: Various additives to dilute, dissolve, and alter products such as dyes, stains, and coatings. Mineral spirits, naptha, acetone, alcohol, and lacquer thinner are just a few examples.

Solvent-based lacquer: Nitrocellulose based coating that is called brushing lacquer. Easy to repair damage.

Spider cracks: The naturally occurring cracks in knots.

Spray finishing: An efficient but expensive process that uses spray guns and industrial coatings to apply consistent and quick finishes.

Tack off: To dust off a newly-sanded surface, usually using a tack cloth.

Taklon: High quality synthetic filament brush.

Topcoating: Topcoating provides the surface texture and sheen of the piece, and is the primary defense against wear and tear. Examples are shellac, lacquer, water- and oil-based urethane, conventional and gel varnish, and Danish oil.

Volatile organic compounds (VOCs): Indoor air pollutants released as gases from many common finishing products, such as finishes, paints, and lacquers.

Wash coat: A light coat done before applying stain in order to prevent uneven absorption. Also done after applying dye to prevent sealer or topcoat (especially water-based products) from bleeding the color.

Water-based coating: A completely clear finish with minimal odor and fast dry time that has the tendency to raise wood grain.

Wood movement: Movement in wood dimension caused by wide swings in humidity levels. Using a film finish on a project helps minimize this problem.

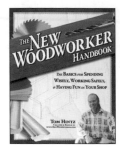